TID BITS OF GOD'S LOVE

Dottie Burdette

WESTBOW
PRESS®
A DIVISION OF THOMAS NELSON
& ZONDERVAN

WestBow Press books may be ordered through booksellers or by contacting:

WestBow Press
A Division of Thomas Nelson & Zondervan
1663 Liberty Drive
Bloomington, IN 47403
www.westbowpress.com
1 (866) 928-1240

ISBN: 978-1-9736-2734-0 (sc)
ISBN: 978-1-9736-2736-4 (hc)
ISBN: 978-1-9736-2735-7 (e)

Library of Congress Control Number: 2018905262

Print information available on the last page.

WestBow Press rev. date: 06/18/2018

I wrote this book with love for God and His children. It consists of thoughts I believe God has asked me to share.

Some of these thoughts are challenging, and some are funny, but all are meant to be thought provoking and to encourage you to look for God's blessings in your life.

I give God all the glory for this book and for anything that may come of it. If only one person is touched by only one article in this book, none of the work will have been in vain.

Please enjoy,
Dottie

tb To Fully Obey

As I sit in front of my laptop at 12:30 a.m., I am looking at a manuscript my heavenly Father has given to me, words He has asked me to publish. Yet I hesitate to push the send key. So here sits the manuscript—not submitted, not published. God has done His part, but I have not done mine. I have not been obedient.

Why? I ask myself. It is not because I can't, because He will enable me to do whatever He wants me to do. Remember?

I can do all things through Christ who strengthens me. (Philippians 4:13 KJV)

It is not due to financial reasons, for God has provided there as well.

So why do I stare at words I know my heavenly Father has asked me to share with others?

Maybe, just maybe, I am afraid to fully trust God will protect me from those who may find fault with what I have written. But unless you fully trust God, you cannot fully obey Him.

And I want to fully obey my heavenly Father.

So.......send.

tb Compromise

The Bible warns us of compromise in our churches. We are warned several times to be wary of false teachers and false preachers. We are told how to spot them and not to believe what they teach, for they will not be teaching the truth. Instead of telling us what we need to hear, they will tell us only what we want to hear—things that "tickle our ears" is how the Bible puts it.

We are to stay away from such people. We are not even to greet them much less allow them to stay in our homes. For in doing so, we share in their evil deeds.

Many deceivers in the world do not confess Jesus Christ as coming in the flesh. They are deceivers, Antichrists.

> Look to yourselves, that we do not lose those things we worked for, but that we may receive a full reward.
>
> Whoever transgresses and does not abide in the doctrine of Christ does not have God. He who abides in the doctrine of Christ has both the Father and the Son.
>
> If anyone comes to you and does not bring this doctrine, do not receive him into your house nor greet him; for he who greets him shares in his evil deeds. (2 John 7–11 NKJV)
>
> These false teachers and preachers will bring destruction on our churches because they bring compromise, and God takes compromise very seriously.

Compromise may not be easy to spot in our day-to-day lives. It may creep in quietly while we are trying to adhere to the rules or obey the laws. I am not advocating breaking rules and laws, but we are to stay truer to God and to His rules and laws, than we are to those of humans. God's Word trumps anything else that there is, was, or could ever be. God is the original rule giver and lawmaker, and His say should be the final say in every circumstance all the time!

While writing this book, I almost compromised. Believe it or not, there are copyright laws regulating scripture—or rather the various translations of scripture. Yes, it's true. Because I am using translations of scriptures and not the original manuscripts, copyright laws limit the amount of verses that can be included in written works.

My first writings contained a lot of scripture, so to adhere to the copyright laws, I began to remove material from the original manuscript. Guess what that material was. Scriptures. Yes, God's Word.

Compromise!

I placed humanity's laws over God's laws.

God told us to spread His Word, and the last time I checked, I could not find where God had put a limit on how much of His Word we could spread. So I rewrote the entire manuscript putting God's Word back in.

My compromise has delayed the publication of what you are now reading for almost an entire year. *Arrg!*

But worse than that, it quieted God's voice.

Compromise costs.

tb What If?

What if one morning you woke up with only the things you had thanked God for the night before? Nothing more. Nothing less. What would you have? A little? A lot?

Nothing?

Forgiveness Vending Machine
Manufactured by the Heavenly Vending Company

1. Little Offenses
2. Medium Offenses
3. Big Offenses
4. Offenses: Relatives
5. Offenses: Strangers
6. Offenses: Acquaintances
7. Offenses: Non-Christians
8. Offenses: Christians
9. Offenses: Bosses
10. Offenses: Coworkers
11. Emotional Pain from Past
12. Emotional Pain Present
13. Physical Pain from Past
14. Physical Pain from Present
15. Offenses: Legal
16. Offenses: Ongoing
17. False Accusations
18. All Other Offenses

Please clearly speak the word *amen* three times into the microphone and press the number beside your selection. Thank you for using the Forgiveness Vending Machine.
—The Heavenly Vending Company

tb Forgiveness Vending Machine

Is this your idea of forgiving? You go to the closest Forgiveness Vending Machine, say "amen" three times into the microphone, press the number that matches your offense, and then *poof!* Out comes the type of forgiveness you need. Nice and neat; clean and painless.

A wise man once told me that true forgiveness requires sacrifice and pain. And he was right. Jesus's example of true forgiveness was not painless nor nice and clean. It was gory, bloody, extremely painful, and deadly.

tb *Can Jesus Put Your Name on This Check?*

Jesus Christ, King of King	**Date: Anytime**
Around the Throne of God Heaven 77777	

Pay to the Order of: The Heavenly Father $ Full Redemption
Full Redemption of Sins Through My Blood for Dottie

Memo: Past, Present, Future Sins Signature: Jesus Christ, Savior

tb Which Came First?

Which came first, the chicken or the egg? I know. The chicken.

> Out of the ground the LORD God formed
> every beast of the field and every bird of
> the air, and brought them to Adam to see

what he would call them. And whatever
Adam called each living creature, that was
its name. (Genesis 2:19 NKJV)

tb I'm So Busy!

My Lord is patient with me. I am so busy running
around doing His work that I cannot hear His voice. I'm
often like a hamster on a wheel that doesn't go anywhere—
just around and around.

Exhausted, I will fall to my knees and cry out, "Why,
Lord, have You not heard my cries? Why have You not
helped me?"

This is when my Lord compassionately smiles at me and
says, "Oh my child, I have heard you many times and have
answered you. You were just too busy to listen."

tb Can't Outgrow

You can no more outgrow your need for God than you
can outgrow your need for oxygen.

Both are critical for sustaining life.

tb Did You Catch This?

And Jesus, walking by the Sea of Galilee,
saw two brothers, Simon called Peter, and
Andrew his brothers, casting a net into
the sea; for they were fishermen. Then He
said to them, "Follow Me, and I will make

you fishers of men." They immediately left their nets and followed Him. (Matthew 4:18–20 NKJV)

Did you catch that? They left their nets immediately. Other translations say "at once" or "straightway." They just laid their nets down by the sea and followed Jesus. They did not go home to say goodbye to their families. Or to pack their bags. Or to put their affairs in order. Or to close their businesses.

They just left everything behind and followed Jesus.

Would you do that?

tb A Man of God

It drives Satan's demons crazy when they hear a man of God singing praises to His Creator, His Lord, His Savior.

I can see them now jumping up and down, banging on the rails of their cages, beating on their chests, or even beating their heads on the walls.

All because one of God's children is singing praises to Him.

tb Forgiveness Jesus's Way

We as Christians are to be Christlike and follow Jesus's example. But because of God's mercy, we do not have to be publicly flogged and beaten and forced to carry our heavy crosses to a place where we are crucified for our sins.

We are, however, to follow Jesus's example in all areas

of our lives even if we find it difficult and painful. And the area of forgiveness is no exception. As Jesus was breathing some of His last breaths on the cross, He asked His Heavenly Father to forgive those who were killing Him while they watched Him die.

Our forgiveness of others is not a death sentence for us; it is a form of worship. It is an outward sign of our trust that God will do the vindicating for us, that God keeps His promises, and that He will take good care of us.

Viewing forgiveness in that perspective seems to take all the sting out of it, doesn't it? In fact, it may even make you feel sorry for those who harm you because they may have to face God's wrath. And we all know what God's Word says about His wrath—it's a fearful thing!

For we know Him who said, "Vengeance is Mine, I will repay," says the LORD. And again, "The LORD will judge His people." It is a fearful thing to fall into the hands of the living God. (Hebrews 10:30–31 NKJV)

tb Lemons

The world tells us that when life gives us lemons, we are to make lemonade. That sounds good, encouraging, but God tells us that when life gives us lemons, we are to thank Him for the lemon tree!

> Rejoice always, pray without ceasing, in everything give thanks; for this is the will of God in Christ Jesus for you. (1 Thessalonians 5:18 NKJV)

tb Which Road?

Which road of life are you traveling? My Own Will Highway? Broad Street? Or God's Narrow Gate Lane?

> Enter by the narrow gate; for wide is the gate and broad is the way that leads to destruction, and there are many who go in by it. Because narrow is the gate and difficult is the way which leads to life, and there are few who find it. (Matthew 7:13–24 NKJV)

tb Power over Demons

Luke 4:31–41 is a must read. It talks about the power Jesus has over demons. By just speaking a word, Jesus cast out demons, who oddly enough, seemed to know who Jesus was. And even more odd, they had to obey Jesus. Our Bible tell us that when Jesus spoke, the demons had to leave.

> Now in the synagogue there was a man who had a spirit of an unclean demon. And he cried out with a loud voice, saying, "Let us alone! What have we to do with You, Jesus of Nazareth? Did You come to destroy us? I know who You are—the Holy One of God!"

> But Jesus rebuked him, saying, "Be quiet, and come out of him!" And when the demon had thrown him in their midst, it came out of him and did not hurt him. (Luke 4:33–35 NKJV)

If demons hear the voice of Jesus and must do as they are commanded, why can't we do the same thing? We, who claim to be His followers?

tb God's Awesome Power

Sometimes, I like to stand in the rain and allow it to flow down on me. I like the feel of the rain and the power of the wind on my face. It reminds me of God's awesome power. It reminds me God can do anything He wants.

He can heal me or not. He can make me financially rich or have me live on just a little. He can provide a beautiful home for me or just a modest abode. He can bless me with a model family or one full of malfunctions.

For He is God! I have very little to say in these matters. It is up to Him. The only thing I have a say in is how I accept what God gives me. Whether I accept what God gives me with thankfulness or grumblings, is the only thing that is up to me.

tb My New Truck

A couple of years ago while I was busy with showing horses and selling tack, I asked the Lord for a new truck. Not just any truck mind you, but a Dodge Ram 3500 diesel with an Allison transmission. That way, I could pull any size horse trailer I wanted to and would look cool doing so.

But it seemed the Lord was saying no. I would ask and shop. Then ask again. Then shop again. The only answer I seemed to be getting was a no.

So being the patient person that I am (*Hee hee*), I waited for a few weeks before asking and shopping again. But there was the same ol' answer—no. Finally, I just gave up and continued to drive my nice, paid-for, ten-year-old truck.

About six months later, our country's economy started slipping into a recession. Business was slowing down. My income was dropping. With expenses increasing and income decreasing, there was no way I could have maintained truck payments. My new truck would have been repossessed, and then, I would not have had anything to drive. Not even that nice, paid-for, ten-year-old truck. God knew this was coming, so He kept saying no.

To which I now say, "Praise the Lord! Thank you, Lord, for a nice, paid-for, ten-year-old truck!"

tb Nicks and Scratches

The Lord has blessed me with a beautiful violin. It is cherry-red tipped in black. The tone is rich and soothing. And He has given me the time to learn to play it. I try to take at least fifteen minutes a day to practice a new technique, a new song, or just to play some hymns. But this constant use is showing up as small nicks and scratches. I try to be very careful with my violin, but there they are— nicks and scratches.

The type of wood a violin is made of is crucial to its sound, so using common household wood oil to hide nicks and scratches is not always an option. Nor is painting the violin. While the scratches and nicks do not affect the tone of the violin, they make it look less than perfect.

But I would like for my gift from God to be as perfect as I can keep it. So what am I to do? Do I store it safely in its case never to play it again? Or do I play it and just tolerate these signs of use?

Pondering this question, I realized that my violin is like most of God's servants. They are all very beautiful because they were created in God's image. At the beginning of their ministries, they had no nicks or scratches. But as they allowed God to use them, to play them if you will, they became nicked and scratched.

But these signs of use—their nicks and scratches—do not affect their effectiveness, their tone if you will. They are just signs of being used for the kingdom of God. However, unlike my violin, once these faithful servants receive their heavenly bodies, all those nicks and scratches will be gone.

So what will you do about your nicks and scratches? Will you put your ministry safely away never to play it again? Or are you willing to continue being used by God and tolerate your nicks and scratches, your signs of use?

Only you can decide.

tb Run!

The next time you fail to witness to people whom God has brought to you—run after them as fast as you can, and when you catch up with them, tell them about Jesus. About how Jesus gave His life for them. About the love of the heavenly Father. About how they too can have the gift of salvation. Tell them all. Make sure they understand before you leave them.

One day, you will be glad you did.

tb We Have God. Who Do They Have?

We Christians have God and His Son, Jesus, to express our thanksgivings to. To turn to when we feel fearful or are enduring painful parts of life.

We also have the Holy Spirit to help guide us along our path. To help us know which moves are the right moves and which moves are not great. Which places are the right ones to be and which ones are not. When to talk and when not to.

As if that were not enough, we have God's Word as our owner's manual. It is filled with wisdom on how to raise kids, conduct relationships, and even how to handle money.

Yes, we as Christians have all this.

Who do atheists have? Those who do not believe that God, Jesus, and the Holy Spirit exist? Who do they express their thanksgiving to? Who do they turn to when they feel fearful or are enduring painful parts of life? Will Satan give them guidance? Tell them the right moves to make? The best places to be?

tb Desires of Your Heart

Delight yourself also in the LORD, and He shall give you the desire of your heart. (Psalm 37:4 NKJV)

For a long time, this scripture was a mystery to me. That was until I realized God is most interested in our hearts and in why we do what we do. He knows that if our hearts are pure and we are seeking Him and His wisdom, our desires will parallel His.

tb Dead Faith

Just as a dead dog cannot fetch, or a dead horse cannot pull a wagon, or a dead cow cannot give milk, dead faith cannot serve the Lord.

tb Broken and Spilled Out

"You were broken and spilled out. And poured at my feet in sweet abandon, Lord, used up for me", are some of the lyrics to the wonderful song "Broken and Spilled Out" by Steve Green.

Broken and spilled out, used up for me. My, how that describes what Jesus did for us. For you and for me, He was broken and spilled out.

Jesus was broken and spilled out at Golgotha. Willingly. Lovingly. Just for you. And just for me.

tb Question

If it takes the faith the size of a mustard seed to move a mountain, will doubt the size of a mustard seed cause us to fall to sin?

tb Fishers of Men

Jesus told us to be fishers of men. But why fishers? Why not hunters of men? Or gathers of men? Or some other type of workers for men? No. Jesus called us to be fishers of men.

And Jesus, walking by the Sea of Galilee, saw two brothers, Simon called Peter, and Andrew his brother, casting a net into the sea; for they were fishermen. Then He said to them, "Follow Me, and I will make you fishers of men." (Matthew 4:18–19 NKJV)

Commercial fishermen go out many miles from the safety of a shore or a harbor. They work long hours at night tugging at large, heavy nets. Fishing is very tedious, hard work. No lifestyle for wimps.

Fishermen often fish in waters that are murky and filled with dangers like sea serpents and sharks. Just being on the water can be dangerous especially when storms come up quickly creating large waves, fierce winds, and deadly lightning. But even in the face of these dangers, fishermen go out and fish.

Some days, fishermen experience great beauty while out on the sea. There are days of calm seas, friendly winds, and baby-blue skies. I'm sure fishermen see sights we on shore will never see, sights that enhance their lifestyles.

Given the dangers they face, fishermen still go out to sea day after day dipping their nets in hopes of catching fish. As they leave the safety of harbors, they must be filled with expectations because they never know what type of catch they will have that day. Then, there is always the ride back to the harbor, which may be discouraging should the catch not have met their expectations.

Do you not see the correlation between fishermen and Christians? Spreading the news of Jesus's love is very much the same. It can be tedious work. It can be hard work. Not the work for wimps.

And it is dangerous to be a Christian. Today, dangers are escalating at an astonishing rate. We are different, and those who are not Christian will not understand us. Remember—those who are not of God cannot understand the things of God.

As a Christian, you will be able to experience some amazing things. Like God's hand moving in ways that those who are not Jesus's followers can never experience. Experiences that enrich your life, encourage your faith, and enhance your walk with God.

As a Christian, you are to get up every day and witness to all who come your way. You are to keep dipping your net into the waters regardless of the catch. Jesus made you a fisher of men; He also gave you your fishing orders.

> And Jesus came and spoke to them saying, "All authority has been given to Me in heaven and on earth. Go therefore and make disciples of all the nations, baptizing them in the name of the Father and of the Son and of the Holy Spirit, teaching them to observe all things that I have commanded you; and lo, I am with you always, even to the end of the age." Amen. (Matthew 28:18–20 NKJV)

So whether you see many fish in your net or none at all, keep on fishing. The soul you do catch is depending on you!

tb So Very Much

God has given us so much. He has given us places to live such as our homes, as well as the earth and all its beauty. He has given us the institution of marriage and other meaningful relationships. He gave us our talents and abilities. He gave us salvation. He has given us breath.

God showers us with a love that never ends. A love that is unconditional. A love that never stops giving. God loves us so much that He wants us to be with Him for eternity, so He created a way for that to happen. He gave us our sacrificial sin Lamb, His Son, Jesus Christ. Yes! God asked His only Son to be our sacrificial Lamb. God gave us His best. His all in all. God did this for you, and me.

What have you given God lately? Your son? Your love? Your life?

Or - have you ever given anything to God?

tb Working from Home

The Lord has blessed me with the ability to work from home. Though I have a home office, my laptop allows me to work from any place in my house. Sometimes, I take advantage of that. At times, a change of location renews our ability to focus.

As I work from various locations in my home, my dogs follow me, and they all try to lie closest to me. Sometimes, they are right under my feet and I accidently step on them.

What if you were in God's house as He worked from home? As He moved from room to room? Would you be attentive to where He was? Would you follow Him around as He moved from the living room to the office and back to the living room? Would you strive to be the one closest to Him? Maybe even sit under His feet?

Or would you be so consumed with napping and eating and doing whatever that you would be oblivious to where God was and what He was doing?

tb The Christmas Gift

A classical guitar. What an exciting Christmas gift! I have really enjoyed this gift and have spent time with it almost every day. I told anyone willing to listen (or pretend to listen) about my gift. I know it was a gift from God.

But as I was playing my Christmas gift, it hit me like a ton of bricks—I had run around telling everyone about my material Christmas gift I thought was from God and had neglected to tell them about a much greater Christmas gift *that I knew* was from God.

His Son—Jesus Christ!

tb Stress Release

Are you stressed? Scared? Lonely? Yes? Then try something like this.

Close your eyes and imagine you are tucked away in a nice, safe place such as the hand of God. Snuggle way down in His hand and allow Him to lift you above your present storm.

Still using your imagination, lean over the side of God's hand and look down at the dark, angry clouds of your storm. See the raging seas being driven by fierce winds and driving rain. Enjoy how safe you feel while sitting perfectly safe in the hand of God that created those winds, seas, and rain.

Start praising God for keeping you safe in His hand. Thank Him for His protection and mercies. Sing praise songs to Jesus for His saving blood. Sing songs of thankfulness for His obedience to the cross as your sacrificial sin Lamb. Sing to God and Jesus with your whole being, with your whole heart. Raise your voice. Sing so loudly that the angels hear your song over the noise of the storm.

With your eyes still closed, worship, worship, worship.

Feeling better? I thought so.

tb The Lynx

My kitty is from a strange breed of cats known as lynxes. She does not look like a normal cat. She has no tail. Her back legs are longer than her front legs, which creates a downward appearance to her body and causes her to look as if she's hopping when she runs.

Along with those less-than-normal body features, my kitty seems to have a fish-shaped nose and a large underbite. But she is my kitty, and I love her.

And she loves herself despite her awkward looks and movement. She keeps herself very clean and well nourished. She is content with the way she looks. She feels there is nothing wrong with looking different from other cats.

The same is true with my two horses. They have different looks, body styles, gaits, colors, and sizes. Each has faults with its confirmation, but they too like themselves as they are. And they care for themselves to the best of their ability.

We humans, however, are different. We go to plastic surgeons for face-lifts and nose jobs. We get tummy tucks and enlargements of areas we feel are too small.

We pay big bucks for Botox injections to reduce the appearance of wrinkles—notice it is the reduction of the appearance of wrinkles and not the removal of the wrinkles themselves.

We may have good personal hygiene and keep ourselves clean and healthy, but most of us dislike at least one thing about ourselves. In fact, some of us will try to change how God made us all the way around.

And then there are those who will not care for themselves. They will not properly nourish their bodies, minds, and souls. They starve themselves physically to look a certain way. They starve themselves spiritually because they need to be politically correct.

Genesis tells us we were made in the image of God. We are also told that He knew us before we were formed in our mothers' wombs. So given these scriptures, do you not think He made us the way He wanted? Maybe we are the way God wants us to be warts and all.

God so loves us that He sent His only Son, Jesus Christ, to be our sacrificial sin Lamb so we could spend eternity with Him. We are that precious to Him. And Jesus loves us so much that He willingly died on the cross so there could be the remission of sin through His blood. If God and Jesus did that because they love us so much, who are we not to love ourselves?

The next time you don't feel like taking care of yourself, or the next time you are considering plastic surgery to change your body style or facial features, please take a moment to consider what you are doing. Please check on your motives for such actions.

If God made you the way He wanted you, are you not then already perfect?

tb Talents

God has given each one of us a gift, an ability, a talent if you will, that we are good at doing and we enjoy. God has given everyone in this world at least one if not two or three talents, abilities, or gifts.

Because God gave us these gifts, they are good gifts.

> Don't be deceived, my beloved brethren. Every good gift and every perfect gift is from above, and comes down from the Father of lights, with whom there is no variation or shadow of turning. (James 1:16–17 NKJV)

I believe God smiles when He sees us using our gifts, abilities, and talents. God is pleased when we enjoy the gifts He has given us. I believe God's heart is touched when we use our gifts, abilities, and talents to help others just because He asked us to.

> As each one has received a gift, minister it to one another, as good stewards of the manifold grace of God.
>
> If anyone speaks, let him speak as the oracles of God.
>
> If anyone ministers, let him do it as with the ability which God supplies, that in all things God may be glorified through Jesus Christ, to whom belong the glory and the

dominion forever and ever. Amen. (1 Peter
4:10–11 NKJV)

Instead of the "oracles of God," the NIV translation
says the speaker is to speak as if he were saying the words
of God. Wow! The words of God!

God gives all kinds of gifts. He gives each of us the gifts
He wants us to have. Some people may have gifts different
from those of others, and some may have similar gifts. But
even the similar gifts will be different, unique. No two gifts
will ever be just alike because God likes variety. Just look
at nature. See how many different plants there are? How
many different birds?

> Having then gifts differing according to the
> grace that is given to us, let us use them; if
> prophecy, let us prophesy in proportion to
> our faith; or ministry, let us use it in our
> ministering; he who teaches, in teaching; he
> who exhorts, in exhortation; he who gives,
> with liberality; he who leads, with diligence;
> he who shows mercy, with cheerfulness.
> (Romans 12:6–8 NKJV)

Note: In the NIV translation, "he who exhorts" is
referred to as "he who encourages."

What gift has God given you? Music? Art? Serving others?
Encouragement? Leadership? Mercy? Administration?
Pastoral?

Are you using your gift to serve others? Are you using
your gift to show God's love to others? Are you using your
gift to praise God? As a way of giving Him thanks for your

gifts? Are you allowing others to see Jesus through your God-given gifts?

Some food for thought: the world calls our abilities to do things talents. God calls them gifts.

The world thinks we are born with our gifts. God's Word tells us He gave them to us.

The world thinks we are to use our talents for humanity's praise. God says we are to use our gifts for His glory.

tb Legacy

Recently, I had the privilege of attending a memorial service for one of my dearest friends. This woman was incredible. Though she had been a Christian for only a few years, she did more in that short time than a lot of us do in our many years of Christian walks.

She had her own quiet way of introducing Jesus to many souls. She did not run around yelling at the top of her lungs about Jesus, nor did she beat people over the head with her Bible. All she did was to walk her talk in her own matter-of-fact but humble way. And God used her. Every time I would say to her, "Wow! God is really using you!" she would just smile and giggle like a girl.

What an example this young Christian was for us much older, supposedly more mature Christians. (I say that tongue in cheek.) She told her husband and her parents that they had to go to church with her every Sunday. The only excused absences involved hospitalizations. And she made sure they were fed between services. What a servant for Jesus my friend was!

She served Jesus even after she had gone to heaven. At her memorial service, when our pastor gave an altar call, another soul answered it and accepted Jesus as his Lord and Savior right then. I'm sure my friend had a big smile on her face and giggled when she saw that. What a legacy.

What type of legacies will we leave behind? Will we still be serving the Lord when we have passed on to heaven?

tb Don't Blow It

Several years ago, I heard a very real voice saying, "This is the beginning of the end." Ignoring the voice, I made no changes; it was business as usual for me. And business was good. Very good. I thought about the voice from time to time, but I did nothing about it.

About two years after hearing the voice, our economy started to soften and my business started to fail. No matter what I tried, I could not reverse the downward spiral my business was in. I now wonder if that voice was God warning me of what was to come. And if so, did I really blow off an audio warning from my Lord? Did I really ignore God's warning of an upcoming slow economy? Was I supposed to close a thriving business before it became a failing business?

Why did I not listen to God and do as I was told? Why did I not heed God's warning? Did my success make me prideful? Or was it just plain old-fashioned stubbornness? No matter the reason, I was being openly rebellious in refusing to close the store. I loved the store and enjoyed everything about it. And I secretly doubted the Lord; I trusted in the store's financial books instead.

My disobedience cost me dearly. It caused me great pain and hardship, and it stripped me of my reputation, my standing in the business community, and my friends.

I found myself in an emotionally as well as a financially needy place. I am sure that things would have been different if I had been obedient to God's warning. If only I had obeyed God.

But God in His great mercy did not let me go through that time alone; He used His children, my fellow brothers and sisters in Christ, to tend to me in different ways. I received clothing, food, and unending love from those who also loved and served the Lord.

I now know what it means to receive gifts I don't deserve. After all, if I had not been so disobedient, I would not have been so needy.

Receiving these undeserved gifts gave me a new look on my greatest undeserved gift ever given to me—my salvation, a gift not to be taken lightly. This gift from God guarantees that we can spend eternity with Him. It is a gift that cannot be earned. A gift that we don't deserve. A gift that no one deserves. No, not one! Our salvation is a gift of love given freely to us, the needy.

Spend time each day on your knees in sincere prayer and earnestly thank God for His plan for your salvation. Don't forget to thank Jesus for His obedience in following God's plan, for His obedience to the cross. Where would we be today if Jesus had been as stubborn and disobedient as I had been? Thank God and Jesus with your whole heart, and praise them with your entire soul.

And by the way, when God talks, listen. You will be glad you did.

> Receive my instruction, and not silver, and
> knowledge rather than choice silver. For
> wisdom is better than rubies, and all the

things may be desired cannot be compared with her. (Proverbs 8:10–11 KJV)

tb The Invitation

Jesus invites you to dine with Him. Scriptures tell you that He is standing at the door knocking. If you open the door, He will come in, and just the two of you will dine together.

Take a moment to think about that. You hear a knock at your door, and when you open it, you see Jesus standing there smiling at you. You invite Him in. The two of you go to your dining room table, sit, and enjoy a meal together.

I wonder what type of dinner talk there would be. Would you ask Him questions? Would He ask you questions? Or would the awesomeness of His presence be more than enough? There you are sitting across the table from Jesus Christ dining with the King of Kings and the Lord of Lords.

Talk about dining with royalty!

> Behold, I stand at the door and knock. If anyone hears My voice and opens the door, I will come in to him and dine with him, and he with Me. (Revelation 3:20 NKJV)

tb Everyone

In Luke 11:9–10, Jesus told us that if we ask for something, we will receive; if we seek, we will find. If we knock, the door will be opened for us. He tells us that everyone who asks will receive. Everyone who seeks will find. Everyone who knocks will have the door opened for him or her.

Everyone. Not just those who are old. Or those who are Goody Two-shoes or always nice. Not only those who live in poverty. Or only the rich. Or only those who go to church every week. But everyone.

Have you knocked on the door lately? Are you seeking Him? Have you asked? No? Why not?

Jesus is waiting for you. Yes, you! His invitation is for everyone, including you. Jesus has invited you to ask, to seek, to knock.

> So, I say to you, ask, and it will be given to you; seek, and you will find; knock and it will be opened to you. For everyone who asks receives, and he who seeks finds, and to him who knocks it will be opened. (Luke 11:9–10 NKJV)

So what are you waiting for?

tb Laws

As I was driving to work, I thought about our government and its many laws. About how the government expects us to obey them all. And ignorance of the law is no excuse.

There are so many laws for just the state of Florida. Add the multitude of federal laws, and an ordinary citizen cannot know them all. We go to expensive lawyers to find out what is legal and what is not, how to do something in a legal manner to be law abiding only to find that even our expensive lawyers do not know all the laws.

Have you been in the office of an attorney? I have. They have rows of books filled with nothing but laws and the cases that brought about the laws. Books that our attorneys use to research the law.

If those who have been to law school have to use volumes of law books to know what the laws say, how can we, ordinary people, know all the laws? And yet our governments from local to federal expect us to obey all the laws even if we don't know what they are.

But this is not the case with God. Unlike our government, God tells us what His laws are. He tells us the laws He has for every life circumstance. He tells us what to do and what not to do and even when.

God gave us His laws in His Word. Our Bibles are our law books of life, our owner's manuals if you will. If you have questions about how to handle something appropriately, see what God's law says about it in your Bible. God tells you what His law says about that circumstance and how to carry it out. God does the telling, but you have to do the searching.

Need some examples of God's laws?

Rearing children—

Train up a child in the way he should go, and when he is old he will not depart from it. (Proverbs 22:6 NKJV)

On friendships—

A man who has friends must himself be friendly. But there is a friend who sticks closer than a brother. (Proverbs 18:24 NKJV)

About work—

> And whatever you do, do it heartily, as to the
> Lord and not to men. (Colossian 3:23 NKJV)

A word of warning here. Once you know what God
wants you to do, once you know what God's laws are, you
are to abide in them! This is where being doers and not
just hearers comes in.

> But be doers of the word, and not hearers
> only, deceiving yourselves. (James 1:22
> NKJV)

Just for kicks, I found a few Florida laws on Google I'm
sure most of us are not aware of.

- Pregnant pigs are not to be confined in cages.
- Corrupting the public morals is defined as a
  nuisance and is a misdemeanor.
- It is illegal to sell your children.
- Unmarried women are to refrain from parachuting
  on Sunday or risk arrest, fine, and jail.
- It is illegal to sing in a public place while attired in
  a swimsuit.
- You may not fart in public after 6:00 p.m.
- Women may be fined for falling asleep under a hair
  dryer as can the shop owner.
- The sentence for horse stealing is hanging.
- The same parking fee for a vehicle must be paid for
  an elephant tied to a parking meter.

- Torpedoes may not be set off in the city of Destin. And it is illegal to lean your bicycle against a tree in a cemetery in that city.
- No one may bring a pig to the beach in Miami.

And people say the Bible is strange!

tb A Gentleman

Jesus is a gentleman; as such, He takes from us only what we give Him. He will never take anything from us. He will allow us to keep as much of our stuff for as long as we want.

But the moment we become tired of trying to hold onto our stuff, He is most willing to take it from us. He will carry and tend to our stuff for us for as long as we want Him to.

I'm talking about worries, fears, and finances. About marriages, addictions, and unsaved family members. About hurts, losses, employment, and health. About your love, praises, time, and character.

Just hand them over to Jesus. He is there patiently waiting to take them from you.

Cast your burden on the LORD. And He will sustain you; He shall never permit the righteous to be moved. (Psalm 55:22 NKJV)

tb Even the Sparrows Know

Matthew 6:25–27 tells us that God cares for the birds; He cares about what they eat and drink. He cares about what they do and how they live. The birds do not harvest crops or store food in barns and yet they do not go a day without a cool drink of fresh water or a meal. God provides for them.

God tells us not to worry about what we are to eat or drink or even what we wear. According to God, life is so much more than what we eat, drink, or wear.

He also tells us we are so much more important to Him than the birds of the air are because He made us in His image. If He cares for birds, how much more will He care for us?

Even so, I have yet to see a bird sitting on a branch reading a book while sipping coffee as it waits for God to drop worms down from the sky. I see them digging and scratching for yummy worms. I see them fly to a stream or a river for water. It is almost as if they know what scripture says about working—those who do not work will not eat.

Huh. I wonder if birds can read.

> For even when we were with you, we commanded you this: If anyone will not work, neither shall he eat. (1 Timothy 3:10 NKJV)

tb A Story Just for You

Have you ever heard of the man (No, I mean a frog) who was placed in a pot of sin, (*Ooops.* That's a pot of water.) The pot was placed on a life—(Sorry—on a stove)—and the burner was turned on low.

The frog stayed in the pot even though the water became increasingly stressful. (Ah, that is, to be increasingly warm not stressful.) Even to the point of desperation. (My mistake— until the point of boiling, not desperation.) And because the frog refused to turn to Jesus—(Sorry, folks–that's supposed to be "refused to jump out.")—the frog lost its life.

Why didn't the frog jump out of the hot pot? Because the increase in hopelessness—(Typo. That's to be "increase in heat," not "hopelessness.")—was so gradual that the frog did not attempt to turn to Jesus and save itself. (Error! That should be "tried to jump out and save itself.")

He just sat there and went to hell. (*Arrg!* He sat there and boiled to death.)

Just thought you would enjoy this story.

tb Do It!

When God calls you to do something, you must do it in spite of your fears. You must never let fear stop you.

Do what you know God wants you to do. Be bold in your faith. Be filled with the Holy Spirit. For God did not give you a spirit of timidity but a spirit of power and sound mind.

If the spirit of timidity or fear is not from God, we know who it's from. Can anyone say, "Liar, liar, pants on fire"?

For God has not given us a spirit of fear, but of power and of love and of a sound mind. (2 Timothy 1:7 NKJV)

tb No Absolutes

Have you ever talked with people who claimed there were no absolutes? No black or white in life? Just a gray zone in which all circumstances must be taken into consideration before a decision can be made? A place where all morals are relative if there are any morals at all?

Yet these same people will know the very second

someone who has morals, such as a Christian, has not acted in a moral way. I find it odd that such people would know what sin is or what morals are, but somehow, they do.

Isn't it strange how at that moment, that gray zone of relativity disappears? How in its place a black and white zone emerges? How suddenly all the circumstances surrounding the sinful act are no longer important? And how morals do exist? At least for those people at that moment.

> There is a way that seems right to a man. But its end is the way of death. (Proverbs 14:12 NKJV)

tb Full Gear

I trust that we all fully dressed this morning. That we put on our jeans, shirts, socks, and shoes. I trust that we dressed for the weather—jackets for the winter and lighter clothing for the summer.

Not to do so would be uncomfortable, foolish, and perhaps fatal. Only someone who is not thinking would not fully dress or dress improperly.

Ephesians 6:10–20 tells us we are to put on the whole armor of God because we are not doing battle against flesh but against principalities and rulers of the darkness—Satan and his wiles.

> Finally, my brethren, be strong in the Lord, and in the power of his might.
>
> Put on the whole armor of God, that you may be able to stand against the wiles of

the devil. For we do not wrestle not against flesh and blood, but against principalities, against powers, against the rulers of the darkness of this age, against spiritual hosts of wickedness in heavenly places.

Therefore take up the whole armor of God, that you may be able to withstand in the evil day, and having done all, to stand.

Stand therefore, having girded your waist with truth, having put on the breastplate of righteousness and having shod your feet with the preparation of the gospel of peace; above all, taking the shield of faith with which you will be able to quench all the fiery darts of the wicked one.

And take the helmet of salvation, and the sword of the Spirit, which is the word of God. (Ephesians 6:10–17 NKJV)

We are instructed to put on the whole armor of God, not just some of it. Putting on less is like putting on just your jeans or shirt when you are dressing for the day. Would you go to work or run errands without being fully dressed?

Without all your clothing, you would not be properly dressed, and you would leave some very vulnerable areas exposed.

And when you dress for the day, do you just take your shirt out of the closet and your jeans out of the drawer and lay them down somewhere, or do you put them on?

You must prepare yourself every day physically with

clothes and spiritually with God's Word. While physically, you must dress only for exposure to the world, spiritually, you must dress for battle. You must! Remember whom you are wrestling with. Satan. The evil one. The great deceiver. The father of lies. The one who looks to and fro for someone to devour.

I am never present when Satan prepares for his day, but I have no doubt that he puts on all his armor so that all his vulnerable areas are protected. He knows he is going into battle, and he intends to win.

That is why we must put on all our armor as well. Every day that God has blessed us with breath, we are to put on all His armor because we are in great spiritual warfare with a worthy adversary. We must dress in full battle gear; without it, we will not be able to extinguish the flaming darts or withstand the wiles of Satan. We cannot stand against the evil one and his schemes unless we are properly dressed for battle.

Did you fully dress today? Not sure? Here's your checklist.

Daily Battle Gear

1. belt of truth buckled around your waist
2. breastplate of righteousness against your chest
3. shoes of preparation of the gospel and peace on your feet
4. shield of faith to put out Satan's flaming arrows
5. helmet of salvation (Thank you, Jesus)
6. sword of the spirit, the Word of God, your Bible (and that means reading it, not just having it)
7. prayer

Then having done all that, stand!

tb Psalm 145

> The LORD is righteous in all His ways, gracious in all His works. The LORD is near to all who call upon Him, to all who call upon Him in truth. He will fulfill the desire of those who fear Him; He also will hear their cry and save them. The LORD preserves all who love Him, but all the wicked He will destroy. (Psalm 145:17–20 NKJV)

The Lord is near all who call on Him in truth. No vending machine prayers here, folks. Prayer warrior prayers!

God doesn't answer some prayers; He answers them all. God loves us, and He will hear our earnest prayers. He doesn't promise to answer prayers that are not prayed in earnest or those asked amiss. But He has promised to answer the prayers that come from tender hearts seeking to do His will. He has promised to answer them all.

God is all knowing, so he knows your heart and the motives behind your prayers. He knows why you are praying. There is no cheat sheet here, no lip service, no conning because God cannot be mocked, for He knows you better than you know yourself.

> You know my sitting down and my rising up;
> You understand my thought afar off. (Psalm 139:2 NKJV)

Do not be deceived, God is not mocked; for whatever a man sows, that he will also reap. (Galatians 6:7 NKJV)

tb You Don't Have to Save Everyone

A wise man once told me I didn't have to save everyone, and he was right.

I am commanded by Jesus to love everyone and bear the burdens of my brothers and sisters, but not to necessarily save them. Sometimes, they are right where God wants them to be.

At times, we think we are helping others when in fact we are hindering their ability to learn whatever God wants them to learn. It is at those times, we must allow God to have His way with them. We are to get out of the way or stay out of the way of what God is doing in their lives and let the chips fall where they may.

How can we know when to jump in and help and when not to? A good rule of thumb is this: when God asks you to do something, do it right away. But if God does not ask you to do something, wait until He does.

Trust in the LORD with all your heart and lean not on your own understanding; in all your ways acknowledge Him, and He shall direct your paths. (Proverbs 3:5–6 NKJV)

tb The Lord's Prayer

The Lord's Prayer is in Matthew 6. Most of us can recite it word for word.

Our Father who art in heaven, hallowed be Thy name. Thy kingdom come, Thy will be done on earth as it is in heaven. Give us this day our daily bread, and forgive us our trespasses, as we forgive those who trespass against us.

Eeek!

I have just asked God to forgive my trespasses as I forgive the trespasses of others! In other words, I have just asked God to forgive me in the same amount and in the same way that I have forgiven others. *Arrg!*

If I forgive others only once in a while, I have asked God to forgive me only once in a while. If I forgive others only a little, I have asked God to forgive me only a little. If I forgive others a lot, I have asked God to forgive me a lot.

But what if I have refused to forgive others? Maybe that certain someone? What then?

Ouch!

tb Obedience

Our pastor has been preaching from 1 Kings; he has been teaching us about Elijah, the widow, and the raven. As I read the scriptures and listened to his teaching, I could see that all three had one thing in common.

Obedience.

The ravens obeyed God and fed Elijah when he was in hiding. Because of their obedience, Elijah lived.

The widow obeyed God and made bread for Elijah using what she thought was the last of her food. Because of her obedience, her flour jar never ran out and her oil can was always filled.

Because Elijah obeyed God, he was still at this woman's home when her son became ill. Thus, Elijah was able to save him. If I am reading my Bible correctly, Elijah prayed over the woman's son to bring him back from death to life.

> Then he cried out to the LORD and said, "O LORD my God, have You also brought tragedy on the widow with whom I lodge, by killing her son?"
>
> And he stretched himself out on the child three times and cried out to the LORD and said, "O LORD my God, I pray, let this child's soul come back to him." Then the LORD heard the voice of Elijah; and the soul of the child came back to him, and he revived. (1 Kings 17:20–22 NKJV)

I used to think that the condition of our hearts was the most important thing to God. But after reading the story of Elijah, I am beginning to think that obedience rates right up there next to pure hearts. It appears they go hand in hand. If God has our obedience, He will have our hearts as well. And if God has our hearts, He will have our obedience.

From what I just read, our obedience to God seems to be a path to His blessings. When God has our obedience, we have His blessings. Now that is what I call a win-win.

tb No Room for Both

I recently had surgery to repair a broken bone. Due to

the tremendous pain of orthopedic surgery, I had to take strong pain medication. While on this medication, I started to believe God had turned His back on me and left me to fend for myself. That experience was very frightening. Fear filled my soul and zapped life out of me.

Reading my Bible and singing praise songs felt like a chore, something I had to do out of duty, not out of love. The Word and the praise songs did not, could not, penetrate my heart as they had in the past.

I was afraid that I would die while God was gone and that I would spend eternity in hell. I was hanging onto an ever-thinning string of faith, a string that was thinner than that in a spiderweb.

My world was very dark, painful, and scary. Instead of praying with the power Jesus had given me, I was whispering—no, begging—"Please God, don't take away my place in heaven! Please God, don't leave me!" I had never felt so much gloom and doom and despair.

I now realize why Jesus told His disciples repeatedly, "Do not fear!" When fear grips us, when fear gets down deep in our souls, there's no room for the boldness the Holy Spirit gives us. Fear and the Holy Spirit's boldness cannot coexist in a soul; it will be one or the other, not both.

So I did the only thing I knew to do—I asked Jesus to please remove the all-encompassing fear that drenched my soul. Every hour, every minute, every second, I pleaded with my Lord, "Please come back and fill me with Your Holy Spirit." I begged Jesus not to leave me alone but to please come back and be with me again. I needed His help badly.

After what felt like years, one day as I was talking to

Jesus in prayer, I once again felt that warm and comforting love Jesus has for me. I felt the Holy Spirit's boldness returning and starting to fill me again. It was just a weak whiff at first, but each day, it became stronger and started staying longer.

The longer I lingered in prayer, the stronger I got, and the stronger I got, the more I lingered in prayer. Funny how they seemed to feed each other.

One of our great hymns has this line: "He was there all the time." And so He was. Jesus showed me that He had been at my side the whole time, even during that very dark, painful, and scary time. Jesus had been sitting there next to me holding my hand as I struggled with my fears and lack of the Holy Spirit's boldness.

Jesus had never left me as I had feared He had. I just didn't know it.

tb From Romans to Timothy

I ran across this passage in 1 Timothy.

> Do not neglect the gift that is in you, which was given to you by prophecy with the laying on of the hands of the eldership. (1 Timothy 4:14 NKJV)

While I have never received a prophetic message with elders laying hands on me, I know I have been given at least one gift from God. We all have.

Romans 12:4–8 tells us we all have received the gift of prophesying, serving, teaching, encouraging, giving, or leading. Romans tells us we are one body with many members who all have different gifts. When we allow the Lord to use us, to use our gifts, we all reap the benefits. The body reaps the benefits because we are one body.

Not sure what your gift is? Where's your desire to serve the Lord? What do you enjoy doing? What do you find satisfying? That's where your talents lie.

Do you enjoy serving others? Find yourself encouraging others when they need it? Is your heart with the children or with the elderly? How do you feel about visiting the homebound or those in nursing homes or hospitals? Are you good at organizing? Love cooking? Singing? Are you a prayer warrior?

Seek the Lord for your answer. Ask Him how He has equipped you for the work He has laid before you. I know He will show you what your gift is and will answer you. When He does, "Do not neglect the gift that is within you."

Nurture it. Grow it. Treasure it. Allow God to use it. And enjoy it.

tb In the Name of Jesus

Have you ever noticed that most Christians will end their prayers with the phrase "in the name of God's Son, our Lord and Savior, Jesus Christ"? Why do they do this? Just as is the case with all the other questions we have about living as God's children, we can find the answer in the Bible.

> And whatever you ask in My name, that I will do, that the Father may be glorified in the Son. If you ask anything in My name, I will do it. (John 14:13–14 NKJV)

Jesus is saying that we should ask for whatever we need from Him in His name and He will do it. Jesus answers prayer requests asked in His name not just to give you comfort or to make you happy but also to give glory to the heavenly Father, God.

Your answered prayers are not only for you to use as testimony about how God cares for His children; they are also to be used to glorify God.

Think about that.

tb The New Year

The New Year is a time of new starts. A time of renewal. And maybe even a do-over or two. We all set goals for ourselves and call them New Year's resolutions—losing weight, eating right, exercising more, or spending more time with our families.

But what New Year's resolutions do we make for God? Not for ourselves as the world does but for our God, who sacrificed His Son so we could go to heaven and live with Him, our heavenly Father?

Hmmm.

Join me in making at least one resolution every New Year solely for the heavenly Father. You know, a resolution like taking on an accountability partner or finding a good weekly Bible study. Or maybe even a monthly visit with someone who is homebound, taking church to them.

Unlike those worldly New Year's resolutions, please make sure you keep God's New Year resolution all year.

tb What Is Prayer?

When researching the word *prayer*, I found the word *communication* most commonly used. I looked up the word *communication* and found such phrases as "the imparting of" or "the exchanging of words or ideas" and "a means of connection between two people."

So should I apply these phrases to the word *prayer*? Praying means I am talking to *and* listening to God, that I am making a connection with Him. I am communicating with God by exchanging words and ideas.

However should I be honest, when I pray to God, I usually do all the talking, not much of the listening. I tell God what I want Him to know. God patiently listens to my every word. When I am finished telling God what I wanted to tell Him, I just say "Amen" and leave without giving God time to tell me what He wants me to tell me. Without giving God an opportunity to share with me His thoughts. I say "Amen" and leave.

That's not exchanging. Exchanging usually calls for the passing back and forth of something. It means sharing. That type of prayer is not passing something back and forth or sharing. At best, that type of prayer is requesting, instructing, or maybe even demanding.

For my prayers to be true communication, I need to tell God what I want Him to know, and then give Him a chance to tell me what He wants me to know. I need to ask God for His guidance and give Him a chance to give it. I need to tell Him my ideas and give Him a chance to tell me His.

I am to talk and then be quiet and listen. That will allow for an exchange of ideas and words, a sharing of desires and wants. It will foster sincere communication between God and myself.

Now that is prayer.

tb Out of the Mouths of Babes

We all have heard the story. A Sunday school teacher asked her class that if she were to go church and Sunday school every week, would that get her into heaven. All her students said no.

Then she asked her students if having lots of money or a big, beautiful house would get her into heaven. Again, her students said no.

Then trying to really test them, she asked her students if she were to do lots and lots of good things for lots and lots of people, would that get her into heaven. Before the others could respond, a young boy said, "You have to be dead before you can go to heaven."

We all chuckle at this story because children often say cute things. But I have found that their statements come from sincere hearts and are sprinkled with a hint of honesty.

In this setting, the young boy was right. We are told that we must die to self so we can live for Jesus. We are told that those who lose their lives for Jesus will also gain life, and that those who hold onto their lives will lose their lives. To go to heaven, we must first die.

That is, die to sin.

> For whoever desires to save his life will lose it, but whoever loses his life for My sake will find it. (Matthew 16:25 NKJV)

tb Spring

Ah! Spring is here. A time when trees and plants come alive. Everything is so green and fresh. Flowers pop with color as they wake up from a long winter's nap. All nature seems to be saying, "Good morning, Lord!"

Oh look! There's a rose growing from what appears to be a dead plant. Why it is even blooming? Let's take a whiff. Yummy! Thank You, Lord, for roses. Isn't it amazing how life can come from something that seems to be or is in fact dead? Life from death? How can that be?

Jesus's resurrection is life from death. Our acceptance of Jesus as our personal Savior is a form of life from death. The moment we accept Jesus as our personal Savior, we become new creations. From the old creation which dies, comes a new creation filled with the newness of life. The moment we accept Jesus Christ as our sacrificial sin Lamb, we move from being one of the living dead to being one of the living—period.

Question. Every time someone accepts Jesus as his or her personal Savior, does Jesus's resurrection reoccur on a smaller but much more personal way?

Hmmm.

> Therefore, if anyone is in Christ, he is a new creation; old things have passed away; behold, all things have become new. (2 Corinthians 5:17 NKJV)

tb The Original War Room

Ever watch the movie *War Room*? It's a must see about the power of prayer and how it can change lives.

In the movie, a woman learns how to fight for her marriage from her knees before God in a room she has dedicated to nothing but prayer. Thus the name *War Room*.

This movie has biblical roots; Jesus told us that when we prayed, we were to go into our room, close the door, and pray to our heavenly Father. This room is commonly known in our culture as our prayer closet.

> But when you pray, go into your room, and when you have shut your door, pray to your Father who is in the secret place; and your Father who sees in secret will reward you openly. (Matthew 6:6 NKJV)

But I have found the original prayer closet, the original war room, in Exodus 33.

> Moses took his tent and pitched it outside the camp, far from the camp, and called it the tabernacle of meeting. And it came to pass that everyone who sought the LORD went out to the tabernacle of meeting which was outside the camp.
>
> So it was, whenever Moses went out to the tabernacle, that all the people rose and each man stood at his tent door and watched Moses until he had gone into the tabernacle.

And it came to pass, when Moses entered the tabernacle, that the pillar of cloud descended and stood at the door of the tabernacle, and the LORD talked with Moses. All the people saw the pillar of cloud standing at the tabernacle door, and all the people rose and worshiped, each man in his tent door. (Exodus 33:7–10 NKJV)

So how cool is that?

tb They Must Obey

Nature must do what God tells it to do. Nature has no other choice for it does not have free will.

Jesus showed this when He calmed the angry waves of the storm. We see this in Exodus when God used nature to show Pharaoh signs of His greatness by cursing Egypt with plagues. Again, we see how nature must obey God in the parting of the Red Sea. And let's not forget about Moses with the burning bush. Or the complete day when the sun stood still as found in Joshua.

Then there is Jonah and the whale. Ravens feeding a man. A worldwide flood. An actual man's hand without a body writing on a wall. Five thousand and more fed with only five loaves of bread and two fish. And many more examples, so many it would take a book to list them.

As we can see from God's Word, nature must obey God for nature is unable to disobey because it does not have a free will, and cannot make decisions for itself. Nature does not have the capacity to <u>not</u> do God's will.

But you do. You have a free will. You have a choice to

obey or disobey God. You must choose to do your will or God's. You were made in the image of God and given a free will by God so you can choose to do for Him what He has asked you to do—to obey Him. Or not.

When you choose to obey God, you are doing so because you want to. Because you love Him. Which makes your obedience and love special to God, for it is genuine.

Your love and your obedience are gifts you freely give to God. Your free will gave you the ability to choose to obey and love Him.

Your free will also gives you the ability to respond to God with emotions. It gives you the ability to respond to God's love and to His requests and blessings.

Should you ever need proof of how your free will enables you to feel emotions, hug a tree. Did the tree hug you back? No? Imagine that.

> The heavens declare the glory of God; and the firmament shows His handiwork. (Psalm 19:1 NKJV)

tb The Excitement of Christmas

At Christmas, the world excitedly anticipates a visit from Santa Claus. Stockings are hung by the chimney with care. Cookies and milk are left out in anticipation of his arrival.

But what if we were to prepare for Jesus's coming with the same excitement we have for the coming of Santa Claus? What would that look like?

Would we put up a life-sized cross instead of a Christmas tree? Hang up palm leaves instead of Christmas wreaths?

Hang small wooden mangers instead of stockings on the chimney with care in hopes that Jesus would soon be there? Would we leave a plate of unleavened bread and a glass of wine in the place of cookies and milk?

Would we prepare for Jesus's arrival by throwing out some of our reading material? Or by deleting certain websites from our computers? Changing the settings for our favorite TV programs? Or taking out the trash that is filled with ____? (You fill in the blank.)

Would we start being more helpful to others? Show more kindness to our neighbors? Hug our mothers and fathers more? Rush out to buy one more Christmas gift? For Jesus?

Would that Bible sitting on your coffee table need dusting? Would you need to put fake earmarks in it? Would a crash Bible study course be helpful? With a side course in prayer?

I have news for you. Santa Claus is a made-up person. Legend has it he is based on a real person, but he is not real. He doesn't have a workshop at the North Pole or elves who make toys for him. And he will never make it to your house in a sleigh pulled by flying reindeer. No matter how long you wait, that will never happen.

But Jesus, the Lord of Lords and Kings of Kings, is real, and He is coming to your house one day. Guaranteed.

tb We All Have Missions

God has called us to handle assignments for Him—missions if you will. And He has given us the abilities to carry out our missions. We call them talents; God calls them gifts.

God also finances His assignments. He will furnish us with ways to accomplish what He has asked us to do. We call this being lucky. God calls them blessings.

tb Bent on Making Me Miserable

I have been struggling recently with some people seemingly bent on making my life miserable. They seem to work at it most heartedly even if it means putting in overtime, as if giving me grief were their mission in life. They say hurtful things, and when I try to talk with them about their behavior one on one as God's Word tells us to do, they turn my words around and make them mean what they want them to.

These conversations seem to always end with the blame for their actions sitting in my lap; they think it's my fault that they treat me as they do, do the things they do, and act the way they act.

I have become very defensive in my relationships with those people and as many would say justifiably so. But that is not what Jesus wants from me; that is not the relationship Jesus tells me I am to have with those people.

Defensiveness creates relationships filled with envy, strife, and anger. We are told that those three emotions are tools Satan uses to fill our minds with garbage and stab our hearts. God has warned us that these three emotions are demonic and cause destruction. He tells us there is confusion and every evil thing, wherever there is envy and self-seeking.

Who is wise and understanding among you?
Let him show by good conduct that his works
are done in the meekness of wisdom.

But it you have bitter envy and self-seeking in your hearts, do not boast and lie against the truth. This wisdom does not descend from above, but is earthly sensual, demonic. For where envy and self-seeking exist, confusion and every evil thing are there.

But the wisdom that is from above is first pure, then peaceable, gentle, willing to yield, full of mercy and good fruits, without partiality and without hypocrisy. (James 3:13–17 NKJV)

When I listen to my feelings of defensiveness and allow my emotions to fester into bitterness, envy, strife, and anger, whom am I serving, God or Satan?

tb Away with Christmas?

Recently, friends of mine told me that "they" were trying to do away with Christmas whoever "they" were. My first response was, "What? They can't do that! It's Christmas!"

What would all the shops and grocery stores do if Christmas were done away with? They could lose as much as three-quarters of their annual revenue if the Christmas shopping season were discontinued. And how about the Christmas tree growers?

During Christmas, we buy gifts and extra groceries, and so we spend more on gas. Why, a year without Christmas would be horrible for our economy.

Eeek! Our economy? Really? Why am I so worried about the economy? What about Jesus? Where does He fit in?

Christmas is supposed to be Jesus based, a season that celebrates the birth of our Lord, our Savior, our sacrificial Lamb. That should be the real reason for Christmas. It's *Christ*mas, not *Gift*mas!

But we have made it a season of running from store to store buying and buying. A season of busyness. A season of gorging on food and drink. Maybe we should call this season *Retail*mas. Or *Busy*mas. Or *Gorging*mas.

How does Jesus view the way we treat the season of His birth? How does He feel about the way we have made His birthday party a season of overspending, overeating, and overdrinking?

I think we know the answer. In Matthew, we see another time when worship had been turned into a time of retail. Here is Jesus's reaction.

> Then Jesus went into the temple of God and drove out all those who bought and sold in the temple, and overturned the tables of the money changers and the seats of those who sold doves. And He said to them, "It is written, 'My house shall be called a house of prayer,' but you have made it a 'den of thieves.'" (Matthew 21:12–13 NKJV)

My reaction to my friend's remark shows that I had made the birth of my Savior all about the buying, the getting, and the giving. It showed that I had been caught up in the commercial side of Christmas and had lost the real reason we celebrate. My house had become a den of thieves.

So away with Christmas, I say. Away with the Christmas as the world views it and as I once viewed it. I want to serve my Lord and properly honor the birth of His Son, my Savior, Jesus Christ.

I want my house to be a house of prayer, not a den of thieves.

> And if it seems evil to you to serve the LORD, choose for yourselves this day whom you will serve, whether the gods which your fathers served that were on the other side of the River, or the gods of the Amorites, in whose land you dwell. But as for me and my house, we will serve the LORD. (Joshua 24:15 NKJV)

tb God's Waiting Room

The room was only one of many in a mansion. It was a cozy room that filled you with that peaceful feeling of home. Along with the wonderful aroma of sweet-smelling wood was the soothing softness of subdued lighting. The wooden walls were lined with people who were sitting and patiently waiting for God to answer their prayer requests.

Some needed physical healing. Others needed their emotions touched. Some were waiting for God to work in the lives of their unsaved family members or other loved ones. Others who had endured lifetimes of illnesses were asking God to escort them to heaven soon.

They were all asking for God to move greatly in their lives. They all had different needs. They were all waiting patiently.

Waiting for God. Trusting that He would answer their requests in His time and in His way.

tb Change

We are told that the only thing consistent in life is change, but we Christians know that is not so; we know there are two things that are consistent in life—one is change, and the other is Jesus.

Isn't it wonderful to have both in our lives? Without Jesus, we can't have true change, and without true change, we can't have Jesus. We can't have the pure, holy life God desires for us unless there has been a change in our lives.

It takes openness and childlike faith in Jesus for true change. And it takes the change that Jesus and only He can give to have openness and a childlike faith. We need to be washed in His blood before we can have true change. Unless we place all our past sinful lifestyles under the blood of Jesus, we will still be living like _____ or _____. (You fill in the blanks.)

But because of the change Jesus has brought, our lives are different; they are much richer than before. We can now understand God's Word. Maybe not His ways, but His Word. We can now talk with God face to face in prayer. We now have the power of Jesus's name in our lives. We now cherish Jesus Christ as our Lord and Savior. And we can now rest in the love God has for us.

> Therefore, if anyone is in Christ, he is a new creation, old things have passed away; behold, all things have become new. (2 Corinthians 5:17 NKJV)

tb Easter

Let's talk about Easter. Most likely, it is not Easter at the time you are reading this, but there is something about Easter that cannot wait.

Last year, someone pointed out to me that Christmas was celebrated more that Easter was, that there was far more fanfare associated with Christmas than with Easter. I agree with this person. Even in the church, I see more emphasis on Christmas than on Easter.

It should really be the other way around; we would not have a reason to celebrate Christmas if we did not have Easter. There would no reason to celebrate the birth of Jesus if He had not died on the cross, was buried, and was resurrected three days later. Unless Jesus lived through these events, He could not have been the Messiah or our Savior.

And Jesus cried out again with a loud voice, and yielded up His spirit.

Then, behold, the veil of the temple was torn in two from the top to bottom; and the earth quaked, and the rocks were split, and the graves were opened; and many bodies of the saints who had fallen asleep were raised; and coming out of the graves after His resurrection, they went into the holy city and appeared to many.

So when the centurion and those with him, who were guarding Jesus, saw the earthquake and the things that had happened, they

feared greatly, saying, "Truly this was the
Son of God!" (Matthew 27:50–54 NKJV)

If He is not our Savior, why celebrate His birthday?

tb A Grandson's Prayer

A dear friend of mine always ends his prayers with "In
the name of the Begotten Son, Jesus Christ." Which is how
Jesus instructed us to pray.

And whatever you ask in My name, that I will do, that
the Father may be glorified in the Son. (John 14:13 NKJV)

My friend told me that one day when he was praying
with his grandson, he overheard the boy ending his prayer
with, "In the name of the Forgotten Son."

Hee hee! Children say the cutest things, don't they? The
forgotten Son instead of the begotten Son.

But isn't that how many people live, Christians and
non-Christians alike? They live as though they are serving
the forgotten Son instead of the begotten Son.

tb One of Those Times

It was one of those times. You know what I'm talking
about. We all have had them. Work is not going well.
Finances are tight. Everything has decided to break down
as the same time. Relationships are strained. The harder
you work, the behinder you get. Yeah, you know—one of
those times.

And wouldn't you know it? Every sermon I listened to,
every radio program I heard had been on contentment.

Really? How could I be content when I was going through one of those times? My needs were great, and my harvest was so little. Every time I had a little extra, an unexpected bill or repair came along. The washer died, or a tire on my car went flat. I mean, come on! I needed clean clothes and a way of getting to work.

These repairs meant money and more money. Money I didn't have. In desperation, I called out to God, "Lord, what are You doing? Do You not tend to Your sheep? Am I not one of Your sheep?"

Then I got it—what contentment really meant. Contentment is not what you have but how you have received what you have been given. Contentment allows you to be thankful for what you have regardless of how little it seems to be. Contentment allows you to be thankful for what God is doing for you now.

Contentment tells you that God will provide for your needs in the present and the future. Contentment allows you to be still and rest in God. Contentment removes fear. (Remember, fear isn't from God.) Contentment allows God to move in your life especially when you are in one of *those* times.

Paul told us to be thankful at all times and in all things. To be thankful in the times of plenty and in the times of not so plenty. When things are going great and when things are not going so great.

Not that I speak in regard to need, for I have learned in whatever state I am, to be content. (Philippians 4:11 NKJV)

By doing the same thing as Paul did, we too can find true contentment. Even in *those* times.

tb Excuses

If you were to take the same excuses people use for not going to church and apply them to other areas of life, you would realize how inconsistent and silly these excuses are. For example, if you were to use your "not going to church" excuses for not taking showers or bathing, you would have something like this.

I do not take showers because

1. I was forced to as a child.
2. People who make soap are only after my money.
3. I shower on special occasions such as Easter and Christmas.
4. There are so many places to shower that I can't make up my mind which one I like the most.
5. People who shower are such hypocrites. They think that just because they shower, they are so much cleaner than others.
6. I used to shower, but it got boring, so I stopped.
7. None of my friends shower, and so I don't.
8. I'll shower when I get older.
9. No shower right now; I'm too busy.
10. The water is too hot or too cold.
11. The shower stall is too small.
12. I don't believe in taking showers.
13. Showering is against my beliefs.
14. (And my favorite): I don't need to take a shower. I'm fine just as I am. I like my dirty life.

tb A Large Oak Tree

LORD is your keeper; the LORD is your shade at your right hand. The sun shall not strike you by day; nor the moon by night. (Psalm 121:5–6 NKJV)

When I read this scripture, I saw a tall and majestic oak tree. Because of its size, it offered a refuge of shade to many not only from the weather but from predators as well.

And I am one of those many. When I stand in the shade of this majestic tree, I am well protected from the scorching heat of the sun and from any predators overhead. However, should I step out from under the protection of the tree, I expose myself to the sun and put myself in harm's way.

So it is with God's protection. If we stand in the shade of His protection, we are protected from Satan's fiery arrows and are in the comfort of His shade. If we venture out from under God's shade of protection, we are no longer in the comfort of His shade and become fair game for Satan and his wiles. Satan will declare that Christian hunting season is open. And he keeps his Christian hunting license current.

My friend, stay under God's shade of protection. You will be much more comfortable there, and you will have protection from predators hunting for those they can devour.

And you will not become a trophy on Satan's trophy wall. Like all hunters, Satan loves to put his trophies on his wall for all to see especially when his trophy is a Christian. What a prize!

So where will we find you? Under God's shade tree or on Satan's trophy wall?

tb Hey, New Attitude!

Instead of asking God why He allows people who have conflicting beliefs to infiltrate your country, town, or neighborhood, thank God for bringing such people to you.

When He surrounds you with such people, He is bringing your mission field to you—no travel needed. No strange customs and foods. No bad water. No passports. And it is a lot less costly.

Hmmm.

Kind of gives new meaning to *homework*, doesn't it?

tb It's in the Letter

Sin. Sing. There's only one little letter separating these two words—*g.* A small letter found between *f* and *h* in the alphabet. On its own, it has very little meaning.

However, when you add it to the word *sin*, you get the word *sing.* These two words have entirely different meanings.

Sinning causes a separation from God.

Singing causes a union with God.

Small things matter, don't they?

tb Pastors

Pastors give their all to us. They show us the walk we should be walking. They teach us about Jesus and how to be more like Him. The warn us of things that may provoke God's wrath. They bring up thought-provoking subjects.

They scold us. Love us. Laugh with us. Rejoice with us. Cry with us. Feel our pain. Counsel us.

Yet pastors are human too. I too tend to forget that, but they are. As humans, pastors need others to be with them during their trials. They need people who will mourn with them, cry with them, laugh with them, and rejoice with them. They need others they can trust with their innermost concerns and bounce ideas off. They need close friends.

Please remember this and support your pastors. Let them know you love them, pray for them daily, and will be there for them if they ever need you. Pastors take on a great responsibility to care for and shepherd their flocks. They have taken on the great responsibility of handling God's Word with care and properly teach it. God holds those who teach His Word to a stricter standard.

> My brethren, let not many of you become teachers, knowing that we shall receive a stricter judgment. (James 3:1 NKJV)

We have a great responsibility to care for those our Lord has chosen to be our spiritual leaders—those we call our pastors.

tb That Glorious Joy

God's promise of glorious joy comes only when you start believing deep down in your gut that God loves you and will care for you. That God will not ask you to do things you cannot do or do not like to do.

Only when you allow your heart and soul to be filled with the Holy Spirit, only when you allow Jesus to sit on your heart's throne can you experience the glorious joy that comes from knowing God is on your side. When you reach that point, you will know deep down that no matter what happens, all will be okay.

And, once you reach that point, you will not fear, because the spirit of fear will no longer be with you. God does not give you this spirit of fear; He gives you a spirit of boldness.

> For God has not given us a spirit of fear, but
> of power and of love and of a sound mind.
> (2 Timothy 1:7 NKJV)

tb The Desert

It is so easy to be critical of those who had to wander in the desert for forty years. Here we are reading our Bibles and wondering how those people could doubt God's mercy and ability to care for them. I mean, after all, did He not part the Red Sea for them? Did He not allow them to cross on dry land without getting their feet wet?

As the Egyptians turned around to flee from Israel, God caused the wheels of their chariots to fall off. And as if that had not been enough, He allowed the waters to return to their proper places and drown all those who were after them. Come on, folks! What more does God have to do to prove Himself? What is wrong with these people? They had witnessed a miracle!

> Then Moses stretched out his hand over the
> sea; and the LORD caused the sea to go
> back by a strong east wind all that night, and

made the sea into dry land, and the waters were divided.

So the children of Israel went into the midst of the sea on the dry ground, and the waters were a wall to them on their right hand and on their left. And the Egyptians pursued and went after them into the midst of the sea, all Pharaoh's horses, his chariots, and his horsemen.

Now it came to pass, in the morning watch, that the LORD looked down upon the army of the Egyptians through the pillar of fire and cloud, and He troubled the army of the Egyptians. And He took off their chariot wheels, so that they drove them with difficulty; and the Egyptians said, "Let us flee from the face of Israel, for the LORD fights for them against the Egyptians."

Then the LORD said to Moses, "Stretch out your hand over the sea, that the water may come back upon the Egyptians, on their chariots, and on their horsemen"

And Moses stretched out his hand over the sea; and when the morning appeared, the sea returned to its full depth, while the Egyptians were fleeing into it. So the LORD overthrew the Egyptians in the midst of the sea. Then the waters returned and covered the chariots, the horsemen and all the army of Pharaoh that came into the sea after them. Not so much as one of them remained.

But the children of Israel had walked on dry land in the midst of the sea, and the waters were a wall to them on their right hand and on their left. So the LORD saved Israel that day out of the hand of the Egyptians, and Israel saw the Egyptians dead on the seashore. (Exodus 14:21–30 NKJV)

But before we get too carried away with our thoughts, let us take a good look at one large contributing factor. Those people had to live that story without knowing how it would end, but we have our Bibles to tell us how. All we have to do is to turn to Exodus 14:30.

And yet we still doubt!

tb Christmas Day

It was Christmas Day, and the weather was terrible—rainy, wet, and stormy. Gray clouds hung low creating a gloomy look to the outdoors. The TV was filled with severe weather and tornado warnings. What rotten weather for such a special day. I wondered what the weather was like in Bethlehem when Mary gave birth to Jesus.

As I was preparing the mashed potatoes for the family Christmas dinner, the lights flickered a few times. *Oh power, stay with me at least until I get the potatoes finished!* Then it happened. I could hear hail on the skylight in my kitchen. Looking out my window, I saw rain coming down so hard that I could not see the back patio. I was suddenly filled with a great urgency to seek shelter in an inside room.

I gathered my dog, my Bible, and my purse and went in the walk-in closet in the master bedroom. I knelt and asked the Lord to forgive me for being scared and to be with me. I heard the roar they all talk about. Fear filled me to the brim. I could hardly breathe. I could hardly think. The roar became louder. The lights dimmed and then went out. I was so afraid. Facing a danger I had no control over, I felt like a wild animal locked in a cage. I cried out, "Lord, this looks like the day I come home!"

Then it all stopped. The roar went away. The lights came back on. The rain became a soft pitter-patter on the skylight. The winds calmed. Physically shaking, I found the strength to thank my Lord for His protection. And I eventually returned to my potatoes.

Later that day while at the family Christmas dinner, I told my mom about the storm earlier in the day—about the wind, the rain, the hail, and the roar. She was surprised to hear about the storm's severity. She had not heard a roar, nor had her lights gone out. Since my mom lives next door, I was confused.

How could this be? Did God visit me with a storm to remind me of His awesome power? Did I need a reminder that only He had total control over everything? Did He need to remind me that He would protect me? That He cared for me? And that He would answer my prayers?

If so, I want to thank You, Lord, for yet another wonderful Christmas gift. One I will remember for a long time.

tb Jesus Will Clothe Them

We all know we are to be modest in dress and be clean.

We honor God by taking care of ourselves and taking care of the beauty God blessed us with.

But we are not to judge others whose dress is not as modest as ours or those who are not keeping themselves as clean as they could. They may not be where we are in that part of their Christian walk.

Instead, we are to help them grow in this area. With guidance given in a loving way, we can help them learn how to dress to honor God and how to use proper hygiene. I have seen the most scantily dressed women become some of the most modestly dressed when they were accepted by a church whose congregants loved them for who they were, not how they dressed.

Jesus changes people from the inside out. Once they know just how much Jesus loves them, they will start to love themselves. Once they love themselves, they gain self-respect that will help them honor God in the way they dress and with proper hygiene. That would never have happened if they had been shunned just because their dress was showing too much skin.

But caution! This dressing thing can be a very dangerous area. We need to keep our dress dedicated to glorifying God or we may slip ourselves. Every day, we must ask the Lord, "Please dress me in humbleness."

tb Living Together as Man and Wife

Adam and Eve were not married in a traditional wedding ceremony followed by a reception. They were married in a ceremony in the Garden of Eden by God Himself.

God made Eve from one of Adam's ribs and gave her

to Adam to be his helpmate, his wife. Not his slave or his maid—his helpmate.

Adam and Eve's union as husband and wife caused them to be one flesh. When God design the institution of marriage, He wanted the husband and wife to be as one and to live as one.

> And the LORD God caused a deep sleep to fall on Adam, and he slept; and He took one of his ribs, and closed up the flesh in its place. Then the rib which the LORD God had taken from man He made into a woman, and He brought her to the man.
>
> And Adam said: "This is now bone of my bones and flesh of my flesh; she shall be called Woman, because she was taken out of Man."
>
> Therefore a man shall leave his father and mother and be joined to his wife, and they shall become one flesh. (Genesis 2:21–24 NKJV)

People who live together without marriage are in a very dangerous place. They will never have God's blessing on their relationships. Nor will they have God's protection for their unions. Though they are just living together, they are really living as husband and wife. They are living as if they had been united in marriage. It is not God's design for the marriage union to be just living together. Thus, they are living outside God's will.

And should they decide to end their relationships, they will have to endure the ripping of flesh just as married people do. Though they were never legally married, they still became one flesh the moment they consummated their relationship, the moment they decided to live as if they had been legally married.

God never laid out a design for the "just living together" relationship as He did for the marriage relationship. Unless God is the designer, it will never succeed no matter what it is.

This is why just living together will never work. And this is why just living together is dangerous.

tb Does Satan Have Your Number?

The Bible warns us repeatedly to be on our guard against Satan, who is always looking for someone to devour.

If Satan were to walk up to you and announce who he was, I am sure you would flee from him or cast him away using the power of Jesus's name. But that is not Satan's modus operandi.

Satan is extremely crafty, stealthy, and persistent. He will wait and wait. When the right set of circumstances comes along, when the time is right, he will move in to attack and devour you.

Satan is not all knowing as God is, so how can he know what our weaknesses are? Where our Achilles' heels are? He pokes and waits.

Satan may move in only a little at first. He will make his move, sit back, and watch your response. If you are not responsive to his poke in that area, he will poke you in another. And another. Poking and waiting and watching. Should you waver even just a little from your full trust in God when being poked in a certain area, Satan will know that's the area he can work in. Satan will have your number.

He will then once again move into that area only a little deeper and using a little more force because he has found your Achilles' heel. For sure he has your number now.

Satan will continue to move in using more force to penetrate deeper and deeper. He has no mercy and will inflict as much pain and damage as he can. Before long, you may find yourself saying things like, "I can't do this because it will make Satan mad" or "If I don't do this, Satan will come after me again."

Now who are you worshipping? It is not God; I can tell you that. But my friend, all is not lost. Get on your face before the Lord and ask for His forgiveness and help. Ask Him to keep you strong in the trust part of your faith. God will help you. He will answer your earnest prayers.

Then you will see things in a different light, be able to see Satan's modus operandi, and will say "No!" Tapping into the power Jesus has given you, you will escape Satan's wiles or tell him to go away in Jesus's name.

There's power in Jesus's name, such power that even demons tremble at the mention of it.

> You believe that there is one God. You do well. Even the demons believe—and tremble. (James 2:19 NKJV)

tb Neighbor's Funeral

Recently, I attended a funeral for my neighbor's husband. He died needlessly in an auto accident in which reckless driving and alcohol were involved. From the fruits of his lifestyle, I believe he died as an unbeliever. At least, his works reflected that he was not walking as a believer in Jesus.

While at the funeral, I saw a huge pouring out of love. Friends were consoling friends. Family members were helping family members. Everyone was mourning with each other. Most of these people appeared to be unsaved souls. But the way they loved each other was impressive.

I thought about how Christians treat each other. We are supposed to love each other with our entire beings. But do we really?

The last Christian funeral I attended was for a sister in Christ, and I did not witness the crying on each other's shoulders as I had at my neighbor's husband's funeral. Nor did I see consoling. Sad to say, I did not witness family members helping family members. *Arrg!* Did not God tell us to do such things? Did He not tell us to mourn with those who mourn? To console those who need to be consoled?

> Rejoice with those who rejoice, and weep with those who weep. (Romans 12:15 NKJV)

But the mourning level at the two funerals was so different. At the neighbor's husband's funeral, there was an intense amount of deep-seated mourning. At times, some of his family would almost wail. But I saw none of that at the funeral services held for my Christian sister. *Hmmm.*

Then almost as if a light had been turned on, I understood why. When we as Christians die, we go to heaven. Our bodily death is just a move from earth to heaven. Death for us means eternal life with God and Jesus, so there is no real need for tears. No real need to cry on other's shoulders. Our funerals are to be celebrations of the one who has finished the race, of the one who is at that time in the presence of God.

> So we are always confident, knowing that while we are at home in the body we are absent from the Lord. For we walk by faith, not by sight. We are confident, yes, well pleased rather to be absent from the body and to be present with the Lord. (2 Corinthians 5:6–8 NKJV)

But funerals for the unsaved are death sentences of eternal life in hell. When the unsaved die, they go to hell, where the worm never dies.

> If you hand causes you to sin, cut it off. It is better for you to enter into life maimed, rather than having two hands, to go to hell, into the fire that shall never be quenched— where "Their worm does not die and the fire is not quenched." (Mark 9:43–44 NKJV)

A place where there is weeping and gnashing of teeth. A place referred to as the fiery furnace.

> The Son of Man will send out His angels, and they will gather out of His kingdom all things that offend, and those who practice lawlessness, and will cast them into the furnace of fire. There will be wailing and gnashing of teeth. (Matthew 13:41–42 NKJV)

A place where the unsaved will be tormented day and night forever.

> The devil, who deceived them, was cast into the lake of fire and brimstone where the

beast and the false prophet are. And they will be tormented day and night forever and ever. (Revelation 20:10 NKJV)

Thus, the friends and family members of an unsaved person who has died have some big reasons for all their tears and for all that gut-wrenching feeling of loss. Their loved one is in hell for eternity and forever separated from God.

Strange, isn't it, how those who do not believe in all that God stuff still instinctively know about hell?

tb Chance?

All things happen for a reason. God has everything planned. If we follow God's map instead of ours. His plans always work out perfectly for us.

Years ago, God gave us a business to run and provided us with an employee I had never considered hiring until my husband suggested her. This employee was not a believer at the time. She admitted that with the innocence of a child.

Although we were in the business world, we were very open with our belief that Jesus was our Messiah. Our Savior. Not pushy about it, just open. We allowed our faith to guide us through the turns and twists of business. We would pray asking for God's guidance when we had to make business decisions. And we gave thanks for the daily income He provided us.

Our new employee saw how God answered our prayers. She saw how God blessed our faithfulness. It was not too long before she started asking us about God and Jesus. And we would tell her to the best of our ability.

She saw how God protected us when a neighboring bank was robbed. She saw His protection from property damage during three hurricanes.

One day when the Lord had protected us from an accident, our employee felt a hunger for God's Word. She started attending a Bible-based church, asked Jesus to be her personal Savior, and was baptized. She began witnessing to her family; she shared with them her new life with Jesus.

About three years later, she was facing death from cancer, but she was facing it as a believer, a saved soul. When death came, she was able to pass into heaven. Do you think that happened by chance? I don't.

Not convinced? Need others?

Once, God placed me in a job that taught me how to use spacing and graphics. (I now put together a weekly bulletin for my church.)

There was a season when God provided free lessons in Toastmasters, a public-speaking club. I now lead Bible studies.

As a child, I took violin lessons for a few years. That knowledge helped me learn to play the mandolin and the guitar. (I now play for my church.)

And while I was in high school, I took a class in creative writing, and look at what I'm doing today!

Chance? Coincidence? I don't think so.

tb Those Who Walk with God

Those who walk with God never walk alone. Though we cannot physically see God, He is there walking with us no matter what. He is holding our hands as He walks down life's path with us. Wow!

> Nevertheless I am continually with You; You hold me by my right hand. (Psalm 73:23 NKJV)

tb The Key

The blood Jesus shed on the cross is the key that opens the door for us to God's throne room. We can approach the throne of God only when we are covered with Jesus's cleansing blood, which washes away our sins. Only that blood can make us clean, righteous, and acceptable in God's sight.

Nothing else can unlock the door to God's throne room, heaven. Jesus is our only key.

> Jesus said to him, "I am the way, the truth, and the life. No one comes to the Father except through Me." (John 14:6 NKJV)

tb *Real* Separation of Church and State

We hear a lot about the separation of church and state. Our government uses this phrase as confirmation of its desire to keep the church out of its policy making and any other arena it is in.

A time of true and complete separation of church and state is coming. We Christians know it as the Rapture.

> For the Lord Himself will descend from heaven with a shout, with the voice of an

archangel, and with the trumpet of God, and the dead in Christ will rise first.

Then we which are alive and remain shall be caught up together with them in the clouds, to meet the Lord in the air. And thus we shall always be with the Lord. (1 Thessalonians 4:16–17 NKJV)

Can't you just see it? You're driving down the road when you hear the trumpet of God, a great shout, and the voice of an archangel. You see Lord Jesus coming down from heaven in all His glory. The graves of those who are dead in Christ open, and their bodies start to rise toward Jesus.

Not fully believing what you are seeing, you pull over to watch. Once the graves have been emptied, you start to ascend to heaven, to Jesus. And you have no control over it. (As if you would want to stop going toward Jesus?)

Jesus's church, those who are God's children, are lifted from earth to heaven. Satan's children are left behind.

Lord Jesus has come back and gathered those who belong to Him and has left behind those who do not. And that, my friend, is the true separation of church and state.

tb Ever Wonder Why?

Ever wonder why people who say they do not believe in God because they cannot see Him will instinctively call out to Him when they are in trouble? They say He doesn't exist because they cannot see Him. But when they are in great danger or in great distress, they will cry out to Him.

Why do they do that instead of calling out to something they can see? Maybe a tree, a house, or a couch? But they instinctively call out to someone who they claim does not exist!

Could those who claim to not believe in God have that same God-shaped spot in their hearts everyone else has? Could God have given them the same need to worship Him as He gave to you and me? Could God have given them the same instinctual knowledge that He exists? That there is a greater, higher being? And that this greater, higher power is God?

tb Worldwide Effects

Genesis 15–16 tells us about a childless husband and wife who received a promise from God that they would have children and thus descendants who would be as numerous as the stars.

But as time went on, the wife became impatient with God and maybe even started doubting His promise. She decided to take the matter of childlessness into her own hands and convinced her husband to have a child with her handmaiden.

The offspring of the union of the husband and the handmaiden was Ishmael. The Lord told his mother that he would grow up to be a wild man whose hand would be against everyone. It is believed that Ishmael is the seed of today's Arab nation and the Muslim faith.

> And the angel of the LORD said to her: "Behold you are with child, and you shall bear a son. You shall call his name Ishmael.

Because the LORD has heard your affliction. He shall be a wild man; his hand shall be against every man, and every man's hand against him, and he shall dwell in the presence of all his brethren." (Genesis 16:11–12 NKJV)

The disobedience and lack of faith of just two people, Sarah and Abraham, had a worldwide effect on many.

In contrast to the above story, we see Mary and Joseph being obedient and faithful to God. Mary was obedient in carrying God's Son no matter what others thought about her. Joseph was obedient to God, and he stayed faithful to Mary and the child Mary was carrying, which was not his.

Joseph and Mary accepted God's promise, waited patiently on God, and did not waver. The Lord told them they would have a Son they were to name Jesus. Because this husband and wife waited on God's promise, a Son was born who would be the Savior of the world. A Son who would save people from their sins. A Son who would be a Savior for those who accepted Him as their sacrificial Lamb. And He would be their Savior forever.

Now the birth of Jesus Christ was as follows:

After His mother Mary was betrothed to Joseph, before they came together, she was found with child of the Holy Spirit. Then Joseph her husband, being a just man, and not wanting to make her a public example, was minded to put her away secretly. But while he thought about these things, behold an angel of the Lord appeared to him in a dream, saying, "Joseph, son of David, do not be afraid to take to you Mary your wife, for that which is conceived in her is of the Holy Spirit. And she will bring forth a Son, and you shall call His name JESUS, for He will save His people from their sins." (Matthew 1:18–21 NKJV)

The doubting of God's promise and the hastiness of just two people, Abraham and Sarah, brought forth a nation of people who have been described as wild. But the obedience and faith of just two people, Joseph and Mary, brought forth a Savior who has saved thousands and thousands of souls.

Though the actions of these two couples were almost direct opposites, they have one thing in common—their actions had lasting, worldwide effects.

tb God's Church

If God feels His church is important enough to send His only Son, Jesus Christ, to die on the cross for, should we not feel the same way? Should we not care for God's home be it a physical building or Christians in the same respectful manner as God has cared for it? Should we not place the same importance on God's church as God did?

Are we not to care for those who are God's church in the same manner Jesus did? For in doing so, are we not being Christlike? Being Christians?

Jesus instructed us to lay down our lives for one another. He set an example on the cross.

This is My commandment, that you love one another as I have love you. Greater love has no one than this, than to lay down one's life for his friends. (John 15:12–13 NKJV)

tb Everyone Quotes Scripture

Even those who do not study scripture quote it. Some say the Bible is just another book, not the inspired Word of God because there is no God. And yet they quote it. They use such sayings as these.

The handwriting is on the wall—

> In the same hour the fingers of a man's hand appeared and wrote opposite the lampstand on the plaster of the wall of the king's palace; and the king saw the part of the hand that wrote. (Daniel 5:5 NKJV)

Pride comes before a fall—

> Pride goes before destruction, and a haughty spirit before a fall. (Proverbs 16:18 NKJV)

If you dig a hole, you will fall into it, and those who roll a stone will be crushed—

> Whoever digs a pit will fall into it, and he who rolls a stone will have it roll back on him. Proverbs 26:27 (NKJV)

When you play with fire, you get burned—

> Can a man take fire into his bosom, and his clothes not be burned? Can one walk on hot coals, and his feet not be seared? (Proverbs 6:27–28 NKJV)

You mean those common phrases came from the Bible? Yeppers! And more.

When people, even those who do not believe in the Bible and all that God stuff, use one of these phrases, they're in essence quoting scripture! *Hee hee!*

My favorite quote is in Proverbs 17:28. It is perhaps the one Bible verse that those who do not believe in the Bible and all that God stuff should practice in their lives.

> Even a fool is thought wise if he keeps silent, and discerning if he holds his tongue. (Proverbs 17:28 NIV)

It's better to keep quiet and be thought a fool than to open your mouth and prove it.

Here are a few other famous Bible quotes.

> A fool's mouth is his destruction, and his lips are the snare of his soul. (Proverbs 18:7 NKJV)

> Do not be deceived, God is not mocked; for whatever a man sows, that he will also reap. (Galatians 6:7 NKJV)

> To everything there is a season, a time for
> every purpose under heaven. (Ecclesiastes
> 3:1 NKJV)

Here is the golden rule.

> And just as you want men to do to you, you
> also do to them likewise. (Luke 6:31 NKJV)

tb New Every Morning

God's mercy is new every morning. Every day you awake, you will find on your pillow a gift from God. A do-over. A clean slate. A new beginning. A second chance. All wrapped in His mercy and given to you because He loves you.

You are not consumed by your sin because of God's great love for you. He is faithful to you for eternity because of His compassion for you. His great mercy you find on your pillow every morning is your gift from Him. Your do-over. Your clean slate. Your second chance. Your forgiveness. Gifts from God.

And God gives good gifts.

> Every good gift and every perfect gift is
> from above, and comes down from the
> Father of lights, with whom there is no
> variation or shadow of turning. (James 1:17
> NKJV)

tb Your Name Instead

> Because he hath set his love upon Me,
> therefore I will deliver him; I will set him
> on high, because he hath known My name.
> He shall call upon Me, and I will answer
> him; I will be with him in trouble; I will
> deliver him and honor him. With long life I
> will satisfy him; and show him My salvation.
> (Psalm 91:14–16 KJV)

What a great scripture! Put your name in place of the word *him*.

Because Dottie has set her love on Me, I will deliver her. I will set her on high because she knows My name. She shall call on Me, and I will answer her. I will be with her and honor her. I will satisfy her with long life and show her My salvation.

Doesn't that just make you want to say "Wow!"?

tb Welcome to My World

Have you ever had a song ringing in your ears? I have. Jim Reeves made popular a great song. The memories of these words floating over the airwaves in his rich, velvety voice is a warm childhood memory that makes me feel all cozy inside like Christmas mornings at grandmother's house or a warm fire on a cold, rainy day.

Jim Reeves was a country and western artist from the last century who sold millions of records. While I am not necessarily marketing the country and western genre, I am taken in by the song's lyrics. They could very well be words from our heavenly Father given to us through His Son, Jesus. Can't you hear them now in the voice of Jesus?

Welcome to My world.

Won't you come on in?

Step into My heart.

Leave your cares behind.

Welcome to My world built with you in mind.

tb How Does That Make You Feel?

How does it make you feel when your spouse spends too much time on someone else? Or gives way more attention to something else other than you? Jealous? Second in importance?

God's Word tells us that our relationships with our spouses are second only to our relationships with Jesus and God. If God places our relationships of marriage just below our relationships with Him, God must take marriage very seriously.

God's Word also tells us that we, the church, are the brides of His Son, making Jesus our Bridegroom.

How does Jesus, our Bridegroom, feel when we give too much attention to others? When we spend too much time with something else? Sad? Second in importance?

We know how God feels.

> I am the LORD your God, who brought you out of the land of Egypt, out of the house of bondage. You shall have no other gods before Me.

You shall not make for yourself a carved image—any likeness of anything that is in heaven above, or that is in the earth beneath, or that is in the water under the earth; you shall not bow down to them nor serve them. For I, the LORD your God, am a jealous God, visiting the iniquity of the fathers upon the children to the third and fourth generations of those who hate Me, but showing mercy to thousands, to those who love Me and keep My commandments. (Exodus 20:2–6 NKJV)

tb I Asked the Lord

One day, I heard someone who had a very wayward life before accepting Jesus as his Savior say to me, "I asked the Lord, how will those who I have harmed in the past accept me? Accept the new me? How will they believe I'm no longer the person I used to be? I've been bad to so many. And the Lord told me that those who are Christians, those who are His Children, will love me."

And he was right. Jesus Christ told us,

A new commandment I give to you, that you love one another; as I have loved you, that you also love one another. By this all will know that you are My disciples, if you have love for one another. (John 13:34–35 NKJV)

tb Like a Pair of Glasses

When I first started wearing glasses, I needed them only to read small print. However, as I learned to rely on my glasses, I reached a point of not being able to read any print without them. Now, I do not see well without them period. It seems the more I have relied on my glasses, the more I need them. The more I use them, the more I have to use them.

Doesn't this happen to us in our Christian walk? In the beginning, we saw only a small part of God and relied heavily on our Bibles to help us. However, the more we relied on our Bibles to see God, the more we could see God. And the more we could see God, the more we relied on our Bibles.

Just as wearing my glasses helps me see more clearly in the natural, reading our Bibles helps us see more clearly in the spiritual. Helps us see Jesus and God more clearly in our daily lives and in the lives of others. Our Bibles help us see how to walk the path laid out before us.

Imagine that.

> All Scripture is given by inspiration of God, and is profitable for doctrine, for reproof, for correction, for instruction in righteousness, that the man of God may be complete, thoroughly equipped for every good work. (2 Timothy 3:16–17 NKJV)

tb Too Busy?

Is your life busy? So busy that you have no time for God? No time for Bible reading? A prayer life? For singing praises and love songs to Jesus? Too busy to spend quality time with Jesus or God? Is your life that busy?

Jesus was a very busy man. His life was filled with healing the sick, performing miracles, feeding large crowds, teaching, mentoring His disciples, casting out demons, and bringing the dead back to life. Add to that the everyday life activities such as traveling, washing, eating, sleeping, and praying and you can imagine how busy Jesus's life was.

And yet He found time to be with His heavenly Father. Our Bibles tell us that He would often go away from others so He could spend quiet, quality time alone with His heavenly Father.

> And when He had sent the multitudes away, He went up on the mountain by Himself to pray. Now when evening came, He was alone there. (Matthew 14:23 NKJV)

> So He Himself often withdrew into the wilderness and prayed. (Luke 5:16 NKJV)

What if Jesus had felt He was too busy teaching, preaching, feeding, mentoring, and so on to go to the cross? What if He had had no time to be our sacrificial Lamb? Where would we be today?

But most important, where would we spend eternity?

tb Poison!

Satan's children cannot stand to be around God's Word because they are Satan's children, not God's children.

Since they are not of God, they cannot understand the things of God; they consider them foolishness.

> For what man knows the things of a man except the spirit of the man which is in him? Even so no one knows the things of God except the Spirit of God. Now we have received, not the spirit of the world, but the Spirit who is from God, that we might know the things that have been freely given to us by God.
>
> These things we also speak, not in words which man's wisdom teaches but which the Holy Spirit teaches, comparing spiritual things with spiritual.
>
> But the natural man does not receive the things of the Spirit of God, for they are foolishness to him; nor can he know them, because they are spiritually discerned. (1 Corinthians 2:11–14 NKJV)

Nor can they stand to be around those who know the Bible or those who quote it. God's Word is poison to them. But they know who Jesus is and fear His name.

> Now in the synagogue there was a man who had a spirit of an unclean demon. And he cried out with a loud voice, saying, "Let us alone! What have we to do with You, Jesus of Nazareth? Did you come to destroy us? I know who You are—the Holy One of God!" (Luke 4:33–34 NKJV)

tb There Were Scales on My Eyes

When those who have been doing the work of Satan accept Jesus Christ as their personal Lord and Savior, God opens their eyes. This allows them to see the sinful lives they had been living before they accepted Jesus. When their past lives are revealed to them, they feel an overwhelming sense of grief and remorse.

While they were living for Satan, they were working for Satan and had scales on their eyes. Satan's scales. Satan does not want his workers to know whom they are working for or how deeply rooted in sin their lives really are. He knows once they know the truth, most people would be appalled. He knows he might lose some of his workers if they learned the truth. He knows some of his workers might start looking at those who are living on the other side of the spiritual fence.

Remember the fence of life? On one side are God, Jesus, the things of God, and God's children. On the other side are Satan, his demons, the things of Satan, and his children. You are on one side of the fence or the other. There's no fence-sitting here. And there is no third choice.

Remember how once Paul accepted Jesus as his Messiah, scales fell off his eyes? When he was knocked off his donkey, the Lord physically placed scales on Paul's eyes. It was only at the time of his conversion that those physical scales fell off his eyes.

> And Ananias went his way and entered the house; and laying his hands on him he said, "Brother Saul, the Lord Jesus, who appeared to you on the road as you came, has sent me

that you may receive your sight and be filled with the Holy Spirit." Immediately there fell from his eyes something like scales, and he received his sight at once; and he arose and was baptized. (Acts 9:17–18 NKJV)

So it is with those who have Satan's scales on their eyes. The moment they accept Jesus as their Savior and accept God's gift of salvation, Satan's scales fall off their eyes.

Once that happens, God allows them to see the reality of what they truly were and who they were working for. God allows them to see the vast difference between living for Him and living for Satan. That allows them to ask for forgiveness and repent for such behavior. It allows them to see God's mercy, love, and power.

Without Satan's scales on their eyes, new Christians can begin to see the things of God they could not see before. They can see the meaning of Jesus's teachings and how they apply to their lives. They can now see the road they are to follow—the road less traveled. They recognize God's blessings and understand how powerful Jesus's blood is.

And they see how much God and Jesus love them.

tb A Stormy Day

It was one of those stormy days. Dark clouds filled with rain hung low. The air was warm and heavy with moisture. The type of Florida weather that screamed "Beware! Storms are on their way!"

While I was on the phone, a weather alert came through. Thoughts flooded my mind. *Is this a tornado warning or just a severe thunderstorm warning?* Looking out the window, I saw the winds were picking up. Anxiety kicked in as I heard small limbs hitting the sides of my home. Trying not to be too hasty with the caller, I took care of her needs as quickly as I could and hung up. Finally, I could check the weather alert, which said, "Brief rain coming."

Really? A brief rain? That was the weather alert? No tornado? No severe thunderstorm? Just some blowing winds and a brief rain? I'm getting upset over some rain? And brief rain at that?

Isn't Satan a bit like that? A bunch of hot air that just blows things around and causes them to hit the side of our homes? Telling all who will listen about false weather reports of severe thunderstorms coming? Doesn't he enjoy pushing that anxiety button with false tornado warnings? Isn't he good at using our life storms to create confusion and fear in our lives?

Well, Mr. Satan, I have news for you. My Savior is a solid ground on which I have laid my anchor. As long as I do not pull it up, my anchor holds no matter the weather.

tb If They Struggled

Jesus's disciples walked, ate, slept, and lived with Him for at least three years. They knew Him on a level we will never know Him. They knew Him as a walking, talking person. If the disciples struggled with their faith as they physically walked with Jesus, so will we.

Knowing this, Jesus sent us the Holy Spirit to guide, comfort, and warn us. Jesus prayed for His disciples.

I have manifested Your name to the men whom You have given Me out of the world. They were Yours, You gave them to Me, and they have kept Your word. (John 17:6 NKJV)

He also prayed for us, who are walking the earth close to 2,000 years after He did. Jesus asked the heavenly Father to take care of us, watch out for us, and help us.

> I do not pray for these alone, but also for those who will believe in Me through their word; that they all may be one, as You, Father, are in Me and I in You; that they also may be one in Us, that the world may believe that You send Me. And the glory which You gave Me I have given them, that they may be one just as We are one: I in them, and You in Me, that they may be made perfect in one, and that the world may know that You have sent Me, and have loved them as You have loved Me. (John 17:20–23 NKJV)

And Jesus made us a promise.

> Teaching them to observe all things that I have commanded you; and lo, I am with you always, even to the end of the age. Amen. (Matthew 28:20 NKJV)

tb What's in a Song?

Have you ever had the pleasure of singing the praise song "Sanctuary"? It's a great song and one of my favorites.
Lord, prepare me to be a sanctuary.
Pure and holy. Tried and true.
With thanksgiving, I'll be a living sanctuary for You.

One afternoon, I looked up today's meanings of some of the key words found in this song and this is what I found.

Prepare—to make something ready for use or consideration

Sanctuary—a place of refuge

Pure—free from any contamination; not mixed

Holy—dedicated or consecrated to God

Tried—tested and proved good, dependable, trustworthy

True—in accordance with

Thanksgiving—an expression of gratitude especially to God

Living—the pursuit of a specific lifestyle

If we used the definitions for the words in the place of the actual words, we might have something like this.

Lord, make me ready to be used as a refuge, free of any contamination, and dedicated to God.

Tested and proved to be good, dependable, and trustworthy and in accord with God's will.

With expression of gratitude to You, God, I'll be in pursuit of Your lifestyle while being a place of refuge for You.

Gives new meaning to it, doesn't it?

tb Which One Do You Do?

When you need to look up scripture, how do you find it? Do you Google? Use your Bible's concordance?

Strong's Concordance? Do you ask someone else to look it up for you?

Or do you even bother?

tb Good Stewards

Remember that God gave us everything we have. Everything. We do not own anything. Not really. Everything we use—our homes, cars, toys, even this computer—belongs to God; it is only on loan to us. We are to be good stewards of what God has loaned to us.

Keeping that in mind helps me take better care of what I have. When I find myself not wanting to do maintenance and repairs on the things God has loaned me, I ask myself, *What if Jesus comes to my home and sees the condition of the things God has loaned me?*

Though this question helps me step up to the plate, there's one thing wrong with it. We cannot hide from God because He is all knowing and can see how we care for what He has given us.

The most important things God has given us aside from His Son, Jesus, are people. God has given us people to love and people who are to love us—Christian brothers and sisters whose paths cross ours for a season and a reason. They are there to minister to us or be ministered by us. They are there to encourage us or maybe discern for us.

God uses people to provide for others, lead others, and assist others. No matter the reason, these people are here for our good; they are gifts from God, and all gifts from God are good.

Jesus told us—no, commanded us—to care for those who are in our lives just as we care for ourselves.

And you shall love the LORD your God with all your heart, with all your soul, with all your mind, and with all your strength. This is the first commandment. And the second like it, is this: "You shall love your neighbor as yourself." There is no other commandment greater than these. (Mark 12:30–31 NKJV)

Jesus did not suggest we love others; He commanded us to.

tb Problem Solving

God will supply your needs and a few of your desires, but you must allow Him to do that. Don't try to solve your problems in your own strength because you can't; without God, you have no strength. Without Jesus, you have no power. And without the Holy Spirit, you have no guidance.

If you are a child of God's, your problems are also God's problems. He cares about His children's trials and problems, and He has the answers to all problems. But you must give Him a chance to send them.

When problems come up—and they will—ask God to tend to them for you. Ask Him to help you. Then do your part and wait for Him to do His. Yes, wait. And *just* wait. God sends His answers in His timing, not yours.

God will answer your requests for help. He will answer your prayers of asking for His hand to move in your life. And He will answer them every time you ask Him to.

You usually have little or no control over your problems and trials, but God does. You have control over your actions, how you handle your problems and trials. And you have control over whom you go to for help and whose advice you follow. Will it be man's, or God's.

So how will you handle your trials and problems? On your own and with your own strength? Or will you allow God to handle them for you in His strength?

With God or without God is the only thing you truly have control over.

tb To Create or Not to Create

Do you have an inner drive to create things? Make beautiful things? Whether it's sewing, crocheting, painting, building, woodworking, or plain ol' gardening, we all have an instilled drive to create things.

I said all of us. Just walk into the homes of those who claim not to be creative and gaze upon their beautiful wall hangings hung in just the right way and just the right place. They will have used colors in a way that creates an atmosphere, a mood, a feeling.

I believe this desire is God given. God created the earth and the other planets and stars. God created all the animals and plants on earth. He created all the rivers, lakes, and oceans. Even the two ice-covered poles.

God created you, me, and everyone else who has existed, who is existing, or who will exist. And when He created humanity, He made them in His own image.

> Then God said, "Let Us make man in Our image, according to Our likeness; let them have dominion over the fish of the sea, over the birds of the air, and over the cattle, over all the earth and over every creeping thing

that creeps on the earth." So God created man in His own image; in the image of God He created him; male and female. He created them. (Genesis 1:26–27 NKJV)

God created man and woman with emotions, feelings, and drive. The man was given the drive to protect and provide for his family. The woman received the drive to nourish and care for her family. But God gave the desire to create to both of them.

God is a creator who made man and woman in His image, so it makes sense that men and women are also creators. Men create such things as cars, roads, and houses while women create meals, clothing, and things for the home.

When you create something, you are fulfilling a desire God has given you. This God-given desire is why you must create something and why you find doing so fulfilling. God gave you that desire as a gift, so enjoy it.

tb The Religious Way of Life

Have you ever thought that perhaps the reason some people do not give their lives to Jesus is because they are afraid they cannot or will not live up to the so-called religious way of life?

We Christians strive for a higher standard of moral living than those who are not Christians. By doing so, we may appear to others as perfect or at least better than they are.

They don't understand that living for Jesus Christ frees them from having to be perfect. They don't understand what it means to live for Jesus. They don't understand that when followers of Jesus Christ make mistakes or sin, they have the ability to be cleansed of that sin. They do not understand that Jesus gave us the ability to repent of our sins due to His cleansing blood. Then, as if a clean sin slate is not enough, Jesus will actually walk with us as we walk through the consequences of our mistake, of our sin. What a wonderful Savior we have!

Please remember that because you live in a fallen world, you as a Christian will be living in the spotlight 24/7. Other people are watching you. Watching how you live your life. Watching and waiting for you to make a mistake. Watching to see if you sin.

Note: Strange how those who claim to not believe in God and Jesus and the things of God know the very second you sin. If they don't believe in God and Jesus and all the things of God, how do they know when you have sinned? How do they even know what sin is?

Allow others to know you make mistakes just as they do. Allow them all—those who are Christians and those who are not—to see you are as human as they are. That you have human feelings just as they do. Allow them to see you are faced with some of the same temptations and trials as they are.

After you allow them to see you mess up, allow them to see to whom you go to 'fess up. Allow them to see there is a better way of handling mistakes and sin. Allow your mistakes and sins to carve a pathway that leads them to the feet of Jesus. Allow your sins to be your testimony of how merciful God is with those who come to Him filled with remorse for their actions. Allow your sins to be your testimony of what life is like when you are covered with the blood of Jesus Christ. What life looks like when you have been saved.

Allow others to see that you are not like the rest, that there is something different about you. The greatest compliment you can hear is, "You're different. Tell me why."

At that moment, you can know without a doubt that God is using you and that your ministry is fruitful. At that moment, you can know without a doubt that you are walking your walk as a Christian living a righteous life.

tb We Are to Pray for Our Leaders

> Therefore I exhort first of all that supplications, prayers, intercessions, and giving of thanks be made for all men, for kings and all who are in authority, that we may lead a quiet and peaceable life in all godliness and reverence.
>
> For this is good and acceptable in the sight of God our Savior, who desires all men to be saved and to come to the knowledge of the truth. (1 Timothy 2:1–4 NKJV)

This scripture tells us to pray for those in authority such as our president and his cabinet. We are to pray for all those who hold offices of leadership or authority, be it supervisors at work or state senators.

I know that some in office do not have the same spiritual beliefs we Christians have. Some in high offices do not support many of our Christian views and ways of life. But nonetheless, God has told us to pray for them. By doing so, we are pleasing God with our obedience. That should be reason enough to include them in our prayers.

However, if that is not enough reason to pray for our leaders and those in authority, we should revisit Exodus so we can be reminded of how God used Pharaoh for His gain and glory.

> And I indeed will harden the hearts of the Egyptians, and they shall follow them. So I will gain honor over Pharaoh and over all his army, his chariots, and his horsemen. Then the Egyptians shall know that I am the LORD, when I have gained honor for Myself over Pharaoh, his chariots and his horsemen. (Exodus 14:17–18 NKJV)

God can and will use even the most hard-hearted leader for His glory. Praying for the president, for our leaders, and for those in authority is a win-win situation. These people will come to a place where they accept Jesus as their Lord and Savior, or God will use them for His gain and glory.

Either way, we as God's children win. God has promised to work all things for the good of those who love Him and have been called according to His purpose.

tb Driving Your Life's Car

You are driving down the road of life, the road God gave you. Sometimes, the road is flat and easy, but at other times, it is hilly and difficult. Sometimes, you can travel eighty miles per hour, but other times, you're sitting at a standstill in 5:00 p.m. traffic. At times, you drive alone, and at other times, you have passengers. Sometimes, you'll have to make stops for gas or repairs.

As you drive down your God-given life's road in your life's car, you will have many experiences, see a variety of landscapes, and meet really cool people. You will drive in good weather with your top down and see mountains for miles. You will also drive in the lowest valleys where all you can see is swamp.

You will drive in stormy weather when your visibility is almost nonexistent. Driving in stormy weather is not a time to start doubting God's ability to get you down the road He has asked you to travel. Not trusting God during stormy-weather drives will have grave consequences. Stormy-weather drives may be when you should get in the back seat and allow God to drive for you. Unless you rely on God during these times, you will have a wreck. *Ouch!*

And - driving in stormy weather is no time to turn back. Only by pushing through such drives will you arrive at your destination. You can't get through the storm unless you press through it. If you stop driving, you will only sit there in your car with the storm beating down on you.

Your storms will not go away just because you want them to or just because you tell them to. Only Jesus can tell a storm what to do.

Nor can you always wait out stormy drives; they do not always go away quickly. Sometimes, they stay for days, even years.

Having to drive in stormy weather can be quite unnerving and downright scary. But if God has asked you to drive through a storm, He has already given you the ability to do so. And it's okay to be scared, to tremble as you drive through gusty winds and pounding rain. The most important thing is to keep on driving and keep on being obedient.

God knows we humans fear things. He is not asking us not to be afraid but to be obedient. He is asking us to trust in His ability to care for us while we are driving through our storms.

Especially when we are scared.

> The LORD is good, a stronghold in the day of trouble; and He knows those who trust in Him. (Nahum 1:7 NKJV)

tb Samson

Judges 14–16 tells us about Samson. Samson was given as God's promise to a barren couple. He grew to be a man of greater physical strength than we can imagine. He did, however, have one weakness—Delilah.

Delilah had been hired by the rulers of the Philistines to find out the secret of Samson's strength. They paid her 1,100 shekels of silver for her spying services. Some believe that could be around $89,000 in today's terms. Not a small wage!

So Delilah went to work asking Samson for his secret. Judges 16:15–17 tells us she relentlessly hounded Samson for the secret of his great strength and used her womanly ways as well.

> Then she said to him, "How can you say, 'I love you,' when your heart is not with me? You have mocked me these three times, and have not told me where your great strength lies." And it came to pass, when she pestered

him daily with her words and pressed him,
so that his soul was vexed to death. (Judges
16:15–16 NKJV)

Day and night, she was on his case nagging him for the answer. Consistently asking him for his secret. She was becoming as irritating as a dripping faucet. She pressed him until his soul was vexed to death. We know what Proverbs says about a hounding nagging woman, don't we?

Better to dwell in a corner of a housetop,
than in a house shared with a contentious
woman. (Proverbs 21:9 NKJV)

Note: the NIV says "quarrelsome woman."

So we should not be surprised that Samson finally caved in and told Delilah what she wanted to know. He had reached the end of his rope and was willing to do whatever he had to do to get Delilah off his back. Her constant nagging had become more than he could bear.

Samson told Delilah what she wanted to know—the secret to his strength was in the length of his hair. And in the end, it cost him his life. Samson endured hardships he need not have endured if he had not shared the secret of his strength with Delilah.

Let us all learn a lesson from what happened to Samson. When we have reached the end of our rope, when we are willing to do whatever it takes to get rid of that something or someone, when we feel we just cannot bear it any more, we need to stop, drop, and pray before we do anything else. We need to make sure that we do not lose our power source. Doing that may prove fatal.

tb My Promises from God

My life-base scriptures are these.

> For I know the thoughts that I think
> toward you, says the LORD, thoughts of
> peace and not of evil, to give you a future
> and a hope. Then you will call upon Me
> and go and pray to Me, and I will listen to
> you. And you will seek Me and find Me,
> when you search for Me with all your heart.
> (Jeremiah 29:11–13 NKJV)

> And we know that all things work together
> for good to those who love God, to those
> who are the called according to His purpose.
> (Romans 8:28 NKJV)

God's Word tells me that His plans for me include
peace and goodness; they will prosper me and not harm
me. His plans will give me hope in a future no matter the
circumstances I am facing.

And God has promised that He will use the bad things
that occur in my life for my good, that no matter the
disaster, He will be with me using the disaster—whatever it
is—for my growth and for the growth of others in my life.

I love God, and I have been called according to His
purpose. God's call, His purpose for our lives, has some
levels of meaning. The most important level is accepting
His Son, Jesus Christ, as our sacrificial Lamb for our sins.

After that, we will find there are levels containing several
missions God has given us throughout our lives. We Christians

are given missions in life—some harder than others, some sweeter, some longer, and some shorter. But they are all God-given missions, and each is as important as the other.

Sometimes, God will tell us what His missions are, but most of the time, He will not. Most of the time, we will operate on a "need to know" basis; we usually do not see the reason for our missions until they are over and we are looking at them in the rearview mirror.

But God's promises do not stop there. God says that if we call on Him and pray to Him, He will listen to our prayers. God tells us that if we search for Him with all our hearts, He will be there for us. If God promised it, He will do it.

Unfortunately, God's promises are not for everyone; they are for those who love Him and call on Him. For those who seek Him, talk with Him, and listen to Him. They are only for those who have been made righteous by the cleansing of His Son's blood. They are only for those who have accepted God's gift as their personal Savior, for those who received the Holy Spirit and have a personal relationship with Jesus. They are for those who know God as their heavenly Father.

God's promises are for His children.

tb The Heart of the Matter

> Change my heart O God, make it ever true.
> Here's my heart O God. May I be like You!
>
> You are the potter, I am the clay. Mold me
> and make me, this is what I pray.[1]

---

[1] Copyrighted by the Capitol CMG Publishing (IMI), 1992, Integrity's Hosanna! Music.

This is a beautiful praise song, one that is enjoyed in many churches. Beautiful melody. Beautiful lyrics. Beautiful song. When you sing this song, it is as if you were standing in front of God singing to Him. Wow! I love it when that happens.

But do you really know what you are singing? If you do, do you really mean it?

In anatomy class, you will learn that the heart is the center of life. Without it, there would be no flow of life-giving blood. No heart, no life. So it is very fitting that God is most interested in our hearts not in the physical but in the spiritual sense.

If your heart is right with God, your life will be too. If Jesus is the Lord of your heart, He will be the Lord of your life. You will lose your desire to live in worldly ways if you allow Jesus to sit on the throne of your heart. When Jesus is your Lord, your King, you will not want to live in ways that displease God. Your actions will reflect that your motives are pure. If your heart is pure, your motives will be also.

Here is another great song about our hearts.

> Create in me a clean heart O God, and renew a right spirit within me.
>
> Cast me not from thy presence O Lord. Take not Thy Holy Spirit from me.
>
> Restore unto me, the joy of Thy Salvation. And renew a right spirit within me. 2

2 Lyrics by Keith Green, Copyrighted by the Shepherd Music, 1984, for the Shepherd Music

Do these words look familiar? They should! Can't quite remember where you heard them before? Here's a hint: Psalm 51:10–12

> Create in me a clean heart, O God, and renew a steadfast spirit within me. Do not cast me away from Your presence. And do not take Your Holy Spirit from me. Restore to me the joy of Your salvation. And uphold me by Your generous Spirit. (Psalm 51:10–12 NKJV)

When we sing this song, we are asking God to make our hearts pure and morally uncontaminated, free of dirt and stain. We are asking Him to reestablish an acceptable spirit between Him and us, one filled with the happiness of our salvation.

God wants us to have clean hearts. Pure hearts. If our hearts are clean and pure, everything else will fall into place. The thoughts of our hearts can cause us to live unclean lives. The seed of sin often germinates and grows in our hearts. That's why we are told to guard our hearts from things that are not pure.

> Keep your heart with all diligence, for out of it spring the issues of life. (Proverbs 4:23 NKJV)

tb How Do You Treat Your Groom?

We are the church, the bride of Jesus Christ, our Bridegroom. Imagine that! The moment you accept Jesus Christ as your personal Savior, the moment you are cleansed by His blood, you became His bride. You were married to God's Son the moment you accepted Him as your sacrificial Lamb. Talk about marrying up!

God's Word tells us that the bride is to love, honor, and respect her Groom and that the Groom is to love His bride so much that He would lay down His life for her. Jesus has already done His part; He has already shown her how much He loves her by having laid down His life for her.

What about you? If you are the bride of Jesus, how are you treating your Bridegroom? Are you spending time with Him daily? Sharing the joys of your life with Him? Going to Him with whatever is upsetting you? Do you thank Him for being there?

Are you following His lead in your life? Do you lovingly honor your Groom? Show Him the respect He deserves? Happily serve Him in any way He asks you?

Are you a wife who fully trusts her Groom with everything from the rearing of children to finances and protection? Are you a bride who believes her Groom is perfect?

Or are you an unloving, disrespectful wife? Are you rebellious? Do you mouth off? Are you argumentative? Demand your way? Pout when you don't get it? Refuse to serve Him? Are you a selfish, unruly, stingy, me-first wife?

As stated before, Jesus has already done His part.

> Husbands, love your wives just as Christ also loved the church and gave Himself for her, that He might sanctify and cleanse her with the washing of water by the word, that He might present her to Himself a glorious church, not having spot or wrinkles or any such things, but that she should be holy and without blemish. (Ephesians 5:25–27 NKJV)

Are you doing yours?

> Wives submit to your own husbands, as to
> the Lord. For the husband is head of the
> wife, as also Christ is head of the church;
> and He is the Savior of the body. Therefore,
> just as the church is subject to Christ, so
> let the wives be to their own husbands in
> everything. (Ephesians 5:22–24 NKJV)

tb If You Have

Do you have food, clothes, warm showers, reliable
transportation, people who love you, health, the ability to
walk, talk, see, and hear, the ability to read this, breathe,
a Bible, a home, Jesus? If you have just one of these things,
you need to praise the Lord! The Lord gave you these
things, not just one of them but all of them.

Yes, I hear you. You have some of these things because
you have a job and can pay for them. But, who gave you
that job? Who gave you the talents required to do that job?
Who gave you the ability to work at all?

Who heals you of your diseases and injuries? Who
allows you to draw your next breath? To see Him in nature?
To hear His voice? To sing praises to Him?

Who placed the people you love, in your life? Who
teaches you how to have good personal relationships with
people?

Who gave you Jesus Christ as your Savior? As your
sacrificial Lamb for all your sins past, present, and future?

God did. That's who.

> And my God shall supply all your need according to His riches in glory by Christ Jesus. (Philippians 4:20 NKJV)

tb Vases of Clear Glass

Christians are like vases of clear glass. Inside these vases you will find God, Jesus Christ, the Holy Spirit, and things that represent God such as His mercy and love. Because these vases are made of clear glass, we can see their contents. Which means others can also see God, Jesus Christ, the Holy Spirit, and things that represent God such as His mercy and love. Others will see what is inside because Christians are like vases of clear glass.

When physical death occurs, the glass vase is left behind. God, Jesus Christ, the Holy Spirit, and the things of God are no longer there because they are no longer needed. The Christian who once walked this earth is now standing in the presence of God. Scriptures tell us that the instant we are absent from our bodies, our glass vases, we are in the presence of the One who formed our glass vases—God.

> So we are always confident, knowing that while we are at home in the body we are absent from the Lord. For we walk by faith, not by sight. We are confident, yes, well pleased rather to be absent from the body and to be present with the Lord. (2 Corinthians 5:6–8 NKJV)

Perhaps Christians are to be vases of clear glass to attract those who do not know God, Jesus Christ, the Holy

Spirit, and the things of God. To allow others to see what God's love and mercy look like.

Maybe the vases are made of clear glass to allow others to see what makes Christians Christians. Unless others can see such things as God, Jesus Christ, the Holy Spirit, and the things of God, they may never know they exist and may never experience His love and mercy.

To show others there is another way to live, another Lord to serve, God allows Christians to be made of clear glass filled with Him, Jesus Christ, the Holy Spirit, and the things of God such as His love and mercy.

God allows this because He desires His children to be transparent, so He can use them to draw others to Him. God allows this transparency, so others can see Him through the lives of His children.

tb Making a Difference

All you have to do to make a difference in this world is fear God and hate sin. When you do, people will notice a difference in you; they will be drawn to you and will want to listen to what you have to say. They will see you have morals and character and live life from a different angle. They will see you are not like others. They will see you are different.

But what they are really seeing is that you have Jesus Christ and His Comforter, the Holy Spirit, with you. That seems to draw them to you. Remember how the people were attracted to Jesus when He walked on earth? Remember why they were attracted to Him?

Some were attracted by the wonders and miracles He was performing. Others such as the woman at the well or Zacchaeus were drawn to Him because He was not like others. They saw something different in Jesus. They saw God.

The greatest compliment you can receive is someone telling you, "There's something different about you. Tell me what it is." Talk about God opening doors!

Proverbs 9:10–11 tells us that the fear of the Lord is the beginning of wisdom. The word *fear* here is not the type of fear that causes one to be afraid, but a little bit of that type of fear for God may help us stay respectful to God.

The type of fear in Proverbs 9:10–11 is the fear that we had for our parents when we were children. It is the fear of disappointing them or making them angry with us. It is the fear that causes us to honor and please them because we love them and because they love us.

This is the fear we are to have of God; it will keep us from doing things we know would disappoint Him. This fear makes us want to honor and please Him. It encourages us to see what God has to say about things. This fear is the beginning of wisdom.

If we have that type of fear for God, we will tend to obey Him, and that's a good thing. Once God has our obedience, our hearts will be right with Him as well.

> The fear of the LORD is the beginning of wisdom, and knowledge of the Holy One is understanding. (Proverbs 9:10 NKJV)

tb Rest

In the words of our Lord and Savior, Jesus Christ,

Take My yoke upon you and learn from Me,
for I am gentle and lowly in heart, and you will
find rest for your souls. (Matthew 11:29 NKJV)

To rest in Jesus does not necessarily mean sitting around and doing nothing while waiting for God to do something. True, at times, we are to physically rest in the arms of Jesus while waiting for God to work. An example of this is when we are sick or injured and need rest to heal.

But sometimes, we are to rest in Jesus in ways that require doing and moving. Times when we rest in Him to help us do the work He has laid out for us to do. Or resting in Him to help us go through a difficult walk.

But resting in Jesus is much more. To rest in Jesus is to have faith that Jesus will safely guide us down the correct path of life while telling us where to go, when to go, and how to get there. It is resting in the fact that Jesus knows the best way to do something and the best path to follow. Trusting that Jesus will tell us if we are to be moving while we are resting or if we are to just be still. It is having faith that Jesus has our best interests at heart and that He knows what He is doing.

Resting in Jesus means walking this path of life trusting that Jesus will guide you, protect you, and provide for you. It means trusting that Jesus loves you and wants only the best for you. It is knowing that He will always be there when you need Him and that He will never let you down.

It is also believing that whatever Jesus tells you is the truth, the whole truth, and nothing but the truth. You can have assurance that whatever Jesus asks you to do, He will equip you with the ability to do it. Jesus wants you to be obedient to Him and to the heavenly Father, God.

It is knowing that Jesus will never be angry with you for being afraid. He will just quietly assure you that all is well while gently urging you to be obedient despite your fear.

He will remind you in words or deeds that Romans 8:28 is true, that all things work for the good of those who love God and have been called. If Jesus has called you to do something, you can do it. Even when things seem to be going badly, God is working out those things for your good.

> And we know that all things work together for good to those who love God, to them who are the called according to His purpose. (Romans 8:28 KJV)

Best of all, resting in Jesus is knowing He will never forsake or leave you. Just like God, Jesus cannot lie. So whatever Jesus promises He will do, He will do.

That is what resting in Jesus truly is.

tb What? Forgive *That* Person? Really?

In the words of our Lord and Savior, Jesus Christ,

> For if you forgive men their trespasses, your heavenly Father will also forgive you.
>
> But if you do not forgive men their trespasses, neither will your Father forgive your trespasses. (Matthew 6:14–15 NKJV)

Ouch! Does this really mean I am to forgive the person who stole from me or lied about me? Who stirred up all kinds of family feuds against me, or verbally attacked me in public? The person who seems to make it his or her personal mission to be rude to me? Or the person who is less than honest with me? Does this mean if I do not truly forgive these people every time they harm me, my heavenly Father will not forgive me? Really?

Doesn't seem fair, does it? I know the feeling, but wait. Listen to this. God sees what these people are doing. He sees how they treat me. And God is no respecter of persons. He loves me as much as He loves those who I am supposed to forgive.

Therefore, I am not to retaliate for those people's actions toward me. Instead, I am to forgive them, pray for them, and place the situation in God's hands for Him to deal with. By doing so, I allow God to step in and take care of the problem for me. I allow Him to heal my hurts and deal with those who caused them.

I don't believe God will send a lightning bolt to strike them dead, but I do believe that if they are children of His, He will speak to them. He will convict them of their behavior or heal them of the pain that is causing them to strike out at others.

And if they're not children of God? Well then, they are just doing Satan's work, and God can take care of that too.

Either way, forgiving is a win-win. By forgiving others, I place them and their actions in the Father's hands. I release any bitterness that unforgiveness may foster, and I will receive forgiveness from my heavenly Father for the times I am rude and thoughtless toward others, for all the times I have thrown others under the bus.

Forgive that person? You bet!

tb We Are God's Children

If you have accepted Jesus Christ as your Savior and Lord of your life, have been washed in His sin-cleansing blood, and have been born again as a new creation, you are one of God's children.

> For you are all sons of God through faith in Christ Jesus. (Galatians 3:26 NKJV)

And God is your heavenly Father.

As our heavenly Father, God has some parenting responsibilities. He cares for, provides for, and protects us. He soothes our hurts, kisses our boo-boos, and catches with His hand every tear that falls from our eyes. He allows us to curl up in His lap when we are fearful. He comforts us when we are feeling lonely.

God delights in our happiness and is elated when we enjoy the toys of life He has given us. He gives us paths to follow and the ability to walk it—the reason for our existence.

God has given us His Word so we can learn about Him and how He wants us to live. It's a book of house rules if you will.

But there is another part of God's parenting responsibilities—discipline. We want to believe God is that all-knowing, wonderful Father in heaven who forgives us each time we sin. That He is the merciful Father who does not hold us accountable for our actions. But that is not God's way.

God has shown us as earthly parents how to raise children who honor, respect, and obey them. If this is how we earthly parents are to rear our children, why would we not expect God to rear His children in the same manner? We reprimand our children when they misbehave or are disobedient because we love them and want to teach them how to live with us. How to live in society. How to be happy.

God does the same for us. That's why we are told to be happy when God disciplines us. God's discipline means He loves us and wants us to learn how to live with Him. It means He wants us to be happy. But most important, God's discipline means that we are His children and He is our heavenly Father.

> If you endure chastening, God deals with you as with sons; for what son is there who a father does not chasten?
>
> But if you are without chastening, of which all have become partakers, then you are illegitimate and not sons. (Hebrews 12:7–8 NKJV)

tb Fear

I was speaking to a sister in Christ one day about fear. Her analogy of fear was that of a darkened room. Because the room was dark, you could not see what was in it or where things were in relation to you. This room was filled with the unknown.

When we are faced with the unknown, our natural response is a fear that causes us to imagine all types of dangers such as boogey men lurking in the dark just waiting to pounce on us. It is a fear that creates great anxiety.

Then someone turns on a light that dissipates the darkness and enables us to see what's in the room and where we are in it. Our newly found vision removes our fear of the unknown and chases off the boogey man.

As she spoke, my mind's eye saw this room filled with darkness. The fact that I could no longer see what was in the room and where things were in relation to myself caused an intense fear of the unknown, a feeling of being lost without direction that caused me to fear. My anxiety escalated to the fight-or-flight level. My fear fed my anxiety, and that fed my fear.

Then *boom!*

The door opened, and there stood a figure bathed in brilliant light that filled the room. In the light, I could almost see who the silhouetted figure was. Almost.

However, I did not need to see who had opened the door because I felt His presence and sweet peace. I knew who the silhouette was. Jesus.

When He walked in, His light revealed everything in the room. No more groping around. No more guessing. No more lack of direction. No more lack of security or safety. All that was once in darkness was in full view. I saw all there was to see. And guess what? No boogey man!

As I stood in Jesus's light, something else happened. His light penetrated my emotions down deep to my innermost being—to my soul. His light rid me of all my fears. My anxieties fell away like a scab falling off a healed wound. As did my blindness.

Basking in the light of Jesus, I saw the things in my room of life in a different way, a clearer way. Wow! No more groping around. No more darkness. No more fear. No more lack of direction. In the place of these negative emotions was a great sense of well-being, peace, and unconditional love.

Jesus was in my room of life with me. His light opened the eyes of my soul. When Jesus walked the earth, He healed many blind men. And I had become one of them.

Standing in Jesus's light, having been healed of blindness, I felt an overwhelming sense of His love, a love that could not be described in mere words.

Jesus's love is perfect, unconditional. God's Word tells us that where perfect love is, fear is not because the love of Jesus and fear cannot coexist in the same arena.

> There is no fear in love; but perfect love casts out fear, because fear involves torment. But he who fears has not been made perfect in love. (1 John 4:18 NKJV)

When Jesus opened that door to my darkened room of my life, He healed me spiritually as well as physically. His light replaced my anxieties with a sense of well-being, security, and His righteousness. He took away my doubts about God's love for me and confirmed my salvation. Yes, Jesus did that for me.

But He is no respecter of persons—what Jesus does for me, He will do for you. The next time your room of life becomes dark with fear and uncertainty, the next time it yields lack of direction, call on Jesus. Ask Him to open the door to your dark room and fill it with His light.

tb Crosses for All to See

Easter. A time of coming out. A time of renewing.

Nature seems to get it even if we don't. Trees show off their new sprouts as young, tender leaves appear. Flowers are everywhere. Their colorful blooms are as full as they can be. It almost seems as if the flowers are all trying to be the first to capture God's attention. Silly flowers! God loves you all!

Lawns are waking up from a long winter's nap with a green color so rich it looks like Astroturf. Animals are shedding their God-given winter coats. The air is fresh and has the scent of newness. Yes, it is a time of coming out. A time of renewal. And nature is so willing to obey God, to do as He asks.

But the one tree that seems to tell this story the best is the pine. In spring, pines undergo a growth spurt that matures into a cross. How appropriate—a cross. And an empty cross at that. This empty cross is at the end of each branch. It seems as if the pine is proud of its crosses and is showing them off. No hidden crosses here!

The new growth that manifests itself as a cross will be the base for more growth that will come the same time next year. A new cross will emerge with that new growth. An empty cross. Do you see a pattern? This year's empty cross is a base for next year's new growth.

It's the same with Jesus. None of us would have the base for new spiritual growth if Jesus were still on the cross. And without new spiritual growth, there would be no reason for an empty cross.

Scriptures tell us that nature worships God.

> The heavens declare the glory of God; and the firmament shows His handiwork. (Psalm 19:1 NKJV)

The more I watch nature, the more I find myself dwelling on this scripture. Which brings me back to those silly flowers. You know, the ones that seem to be competing for God's attention. Are they truly competing for the attention of God? Or are they worshipping God?

Either way, at least they know whose attention to bid for. And they know whom to worship!

tb There Is None—No, Not One

> There is none righteous, no not one; there is none who understands; there is none who seeks after God. They have all turned aside; they have together become unprofitable; there is none who does good, no, not one. (Romans 3:10–12 NKJV)

Wow! Does this not sound like our America or what?

Our country has slowly but most assuredly turned away from God and His ways. There is no room for prayer or scriptures, for Jesus or the Holy Spirit, for God or for the things of God in our public schools, in our government settings, and in other public venues. We have turned from God's teachings such as:

1. *Children are blessings from God.* But we consider them inconveniences that should be disposed of, something worthless.

2. *Treat your neighbor as yourself.* Today, most people in our country live with that me-first philosophy—dog eat dog, look out for number one, give others lots of empty niceties but no real loyalty. That seems common and the normal way of life.

3. *Do not worship any idols. For I am a jealous God.* But most of our fellow citizens worship the almighty dollar instead of the almighty God. They put money and the things of money way ahead of God and the things of God. They idolize money and the power that comes with it.

However, all is not lost, my fellow Christians, because God has given us this promise.

> When I shut up heaven and there is no rain, or command the locusts to devour the land, or send pestilence among My people, if My people who are called by My name will humble themselves and pray and seek My face, and turn from their wicked ways, then I will hear from heaven, and will forgive their sin and heal their land. (2 Chronicles 7:13–14 NKJV)

God promised that when He sends locusts, droughts, and the like, if those who are called by His name, Christians, will turn from their wicked ways and sinful lifestyles and seek Him with true humility and prayer, He will hear their prayers and heal their land.

And God always keeps His promises.

tb What Is Love?

We are told in Corinthians that of faith, hope, and love, love is the greatest. But what else can we say about love?

Love is contagious—
Show love to a cat and you get a love song; to a dog and you get a wagging tail.

Love is powerful—
Unconditional love for others can help them through trials. It gives strength and courage to those who need it.

Love is medicine—
A kind word delivered in love is music to the soul. It will lift you up out of the darkest of mires. It gives hope when there seems to be none.

Love is a motivator—
Love is why dads work twelve-hour days to provide for their families and why moms rock their young children all night.

Love is patient—

It is why we continue to help others until they can help themselves.

Love is a shield—

It is why a brother warns another brother of impending doom and why we risk close relationships.

Love is a mark of God's children—

It sets us apart from the world. We are told to love one another so the world will see we are different.

Love saves—

It is why people will risk their lives to save that of another.

Love redeems—

Love is the motivator behind forgiveness.

Love gave us our salvation—

Because of His great love for us, Jesus willingly went to the cross and died for sins He had never committed—sins of the past and sins of the future. Your sins and my sins. As the song says, He had 12,000 angels at His beck and call who would have saved Him had He asked them to, but He stayed on the cross until it was finished.

Love is why God gave us Jesus and salvation and why we tell others about Jesus. God's Word is true. Out of faith, hope and love, love is the greatest.

> And now abide faith, hope, love, these three; but the greatest of these is love. (1 Corinthians 13:13 NKJV)

tb Repay No One Evil for Evil

When someone harms you, Jesus instructs you to forgive that person. This is not a suggestion; it is an instruction. A command if you will. So please forgive that person, truly forgive, and pray for him or her. In doing so, you will place that person in the hands of God.

True forgiveness is not worrying about what those who offend you will do or say about you. It is not having to get even with them or having to be the first to tell your story so others will know your version. Nor is it treating them badly just because that's the way they treated you or ignoring them because you don't like how they acted.

No! True forgiveness is having faith and trust in God's ability and willingness to take care of the situation for you. It is the type of faith that helps you place them in God's hands and leave them there. It is having enough faith and trust in God's ability and willingness to care for you that you do not have to treat the other person negatively.

True forgiveness is having the faith that allows you to put the situation in God's hands, step back, and allow Him to handle the situation as and when He chooses.

True forgiveness is having faith in God's desire to do good for you and in the fact He will take care of you. You are God's child, and He knows how to take care of His children. He will protect you. He will vindicate you. He will avenge you should the need arise.

And He will do so in a way that shows your innocence and His great power, a way that will bring glory to Himself and to His Son, Jesus. In a way that shows just how much He loves you.

Repay no one evil for evil. Have regard for good things in the sight of all men. If it is possible, as much as depends on you, live peaceably with all men.

Beloved, do not avenge yourselves, but rather give place to wrath; for it is written, "Vengeance is Mine, I will repay." says the Lord. (Romans 12:17–19 NKJV)

tb *Your* Lord Is

Whatever and whoever determines …

- what you wear,
- what you eat,
- where you sleep,
- what you drive,
- where you go,
- where and why you work,
- what you spend your money on,
- how you handle your money and your bills,
- where and how you live,
- the movies you watch,
- the music you listen to,
- how you spend your time,
- how you treat your parents,
- how you handle your relationships,
- what you read,
- whom you turn to when you need answers or help, and
- where you will be after you die

Who the lord of your life is will determine your choices in those areas no matter what or who it is. If it controls how or why you make your choices in life, it is the lord of your life.

Is the Lord who controls your life Jesus? Is your Lord the Lord of Lords and the King of Kings? Or is it something or someone else?

Jesus is the only Lord

- you can trust,
- who will be there for you,
- who will be honest with you,
- who can truly help you,
- who cares about what happens to you,
- who loves you deeply, and
- who willingly died for you.

There is one more reason you should have Jesus as the Lord of your life. All the things listed at the beginning of this article are not permanent; they are all temporary.

But Jesus is forever.

Jesus Christ is the same yesterday, today and forever. (Hebrews 13:8 NKJV)

tb Have I Remembered Everyone?

Now let's see. I have prayed for

- my husband,
- my parents,
- my children,
- my sisters,

- my brothers,
- my pastor and his family,
- my church,
- those who need a touch from God,
- the sick,
- the injured,
- missionaries,
- those who are in a trial,
- unsaved loved ones who do not know Jesus, and
- God's guidance in my day.

And I have given thanks

- to God for His Son, Jesus, my sacrificial sin Lamb,
- to Jesus for His obedience to the cross, and
- to God for His mercy toward me and His answers to my prayers.

Hmmm. Looks like I've covered everything, Lord. Is there anything or anyone else I need to pray for?

Therefore I exhort first of all that supplications, prayers, intercessions, and giving of thanks be made for all men, for kings and all who are in authority, that we may lead a quiet and peaceable life in all godliness and reverence. (1 Timothy 2:1–2 NKJV)

For all men and kings and all who are in authority? Does this mean I'm supposed to pray for people such as our country's president? Our mayor? Others in public office? Even if I don't agree with them? Even if they're doing things that aren't biblical? For those who believe in and are living lives that You, Lord, have told me are sinful? For those people too, Lord?

For this is good and acceptable in the sight of God our

Savior, who desires all men to be saved and to come to the knowledge of the truth. (1 Timothy 2:3–4 NKJV)

Okay, Lord, I'll pray for all those who hold public offices from the president of the United States down to my county commissioner.

tb Heavenly Fathers

Have you ever wondered why God is referred as He, Him, and His?

Disclaimer: I am in no way a woman libber, a man libber, or any kind of libber. Women are women and men are men, and they have their roles in life respectively.

But all throughout the Bible, God is referred to as He, His, or Him. We are told several times that God is our heavenly Father. Jesus said such things as, "If you see me, you have seen the Father" and "my Father who is in heaven."

But why father? Why not mother? Mothers tend to be more nurturing, more tender than fathers. Mothers are usually given the task of tending to the children and usually have a sixth sense about their needs. We are referred to as the children of God, so again I ask, why not mothers?

Being children of God means that we are collectively known as God's family; God is known as the heavenly Father of His family. So let us look at the many roles a father holds in a family.

Fathers are the spiritual leaders of their households. They are to teach their children about God and about the things of God.

Fathers are the providers for their families and the protectors of their households.

Fathers are to have compassion for their children. Their strong arms are to lovingly hold their children anytime the need arises. Fathers are to help their children feel safe, loved, and protected. They are to be problem solvers.

Fathers are to discipline their children when they misbehave. They are to encourage their children when they behave. Fathers are to have mercy and show their family unconditional love regardless of their behavior.

Fathers are to be cheerleaders for their children. Giving them a big ol' hearty "Atta boy!" when his children try their best.

Fathers should enjoy giving their children gifts and lovingly tend to their families' needs before their own. They are to go with less to meet the needs of their families or so their families can have that special something.

Fathers are to spend time with their families. They should love family time, a time to listen to the concerns, sorrows, and hurts of their children and lovingly give advice on how to handle those concerns, sorrows, and hurts.

Fathers will drop everything when a family member calls out for help. They will be there when needed every time.

Wow! Doesn't that sound just like our heavenly Father? Can you not see how the heart of a godly human father reflects the heart of our heavenly Father? No wonder God is referred to in the male gender.

Now I understand.

Do not call anyone on earth your father,
for One is your Father, He is in heaven.
(Matthew 23:9 NKJV)

tb New Starts

The New Year. New beginnings in life. A time of firsts. You have had lots of them in your life—your first birthday, first day in school, first bike ride, first real friend, first date, first movie at the theater, first time driving, first job, first day as Mr. and Mrs. The list goes on.

All these firsts were exhilarating, times when your felt very alive, times that reverberated with excitement!

But do you remember your first day as a Christian? You were so filled with God's greatness, mercy, and love that you just had to share it, and share it you did. You shared it with anyone who would listen. And with some who didn't.

How is your life with Jesus today? Is it still new? Still exciting? Still alive with that reverberating excitement? Or has the newness worn off?

Why not take this time to have your own personal new year with your Savior? A time when you reignite that love flame for Jesus? A time of rededicating your life, love, and heart to your Lord?

If you find that your life with the Lord does not have that same lure or your walk does not have that same skip, take advantage of the new year to resolve to return to your first love, Jesus. It will be the best New Year's resolution you will ever make.

tb A Flashlight

Then Jesus spoke to them again saying, "I am the light of the world. He who follows

Me shall not walk in darkness, but have the light of life." (John 8:12 NKJV)

Jesus told us that He was the light of the world and that whoever followed Him would have the light of life. How is your light? Is it strong or dim? Does your flashlight need repairs or a new power supply?

A dim flashlight is of little use; it is only slightly better than none at all. You can do only two things with a dim flashlight—throw it away or recharge the battery.

So it is with our spiritual light; at times, it needs a recharge. Do not allow the lack of Bible study and prayer time to drain your battery. Spend time every day in God's Word and on your knees in God's presence in prayer.

Keep your spiritual light bright and strong by keeping your spiritual battery charged. A bright spiritual light helps you see as you walk your spiritual path, and it will help others see your light as well.

You never know when your strong spiritual light may help others who have lost their way—those whose light has become so dim that they have wandered off the narrow path onto the broad one.

Your strong spiritual light may be the light that allows others to find their way to Jesus.

tb A Christmas Gift

God has given us so much—a beautiful earth and all its beauty, the institution of marriage, the ability to have meaningful relationships, the blessings of parenthood, and so much more.

God showers us with eternal, unconditional love beyond our greatest imagination.

God's desire to be with us is so great that He gave His all—His Son—to be our sacrificial Lamb.

God did that for you and me because He wants us to live in heaven, where He has prepared a place for us, for eternity. God, the almighty Creator of all that exists, did this for you and me.

What have you given to God as an expression of your love for Him?

Or have you ever given anything to God?

Why don't you give God your all this Christmas? What's stopping you from wrapping your heart and love in your worship and putting a bow of kisses on top?

Present it to God and Jesus as your Christmas gift to them. What better Christmas gift could you give them than your heart and love?

After all, they gave you theirs first.

tb An All-Consuming Fire

In a recent fire, two young innocent twins died. The thought of their little bodies being consumed by fire is gruesome to imagine. The fire burned everything in their home as well.

Fire can provide warmth and light. It can cook our food. But fire can also be dangerous. Unattended fires can grow from a little flicker to a raging monster ravishing everything in its way.

Fire is an equal-opportunity destroyer. Appearing to have a mind of its own, it goes where and when it wants to. And we can be at its mercy. No matter the amount of water or foam sprayed on a fire, it will continue on its mission of destruction given just the smallest of chances. Only once the entire area is consumed or drenched will the fire be stopped.

And so it is with sin in our lives that we do not keep in check. If you do not listen to the Holy Spirit's warnings as you walk your Christian walk, if you do not stay close to Jesus Christ and allow Him to catch you when you stumble, your sins will be just like that fire. If left unattended, they both start as small sparks and grow into raging monsters that will consume you.

The unchecked sin you have not repented of will seem to have a mind of its own. It will violently rage in your soul and eat away at anything that is of God. No matter how hard you try not to sin, you will sin over and over. Your unchecked sin will destroy you and all that stands between you and that sin just as that fire destroyed everything in its way including those sweet twins.

Try as you might, you can't put this fire out; only the Word of God and the blood of Jesus can.

tb Peace

Peace. We all want it. All peoples. All religions. All nationalities.

In the 1960s, a generation was seeking peace. Peace symbols. Peace signs. Peaceful but rebellious rioting against the establishment in the name of peace. (Is not peace-seeking rioters an oxymoron?) This search for peace compelled a generation to openly question the establishment. The desire for peace was strong.

I can tell you where you can find peace and how to obtain it—by accepting God's Son, Jesus Christ, as your personal Savior and by trusting in God. There is no need for violence, or special clothing, or signs, or riots. Only a bent knee and an honest desire to accept God's gift of salvation is needed.

The peace you receive from Jesus will not safeguard you from the problems and trials life lays at your feet, but the peace you receive from Jesus will help you through all those problems and trials.

The peace that comes from personally knowing Jesus as your Savior will transcend your understanding.

So how about it? Put down that peace sign, throw away the peace T-shirt, and trade in your riot gear. In place of such things, put on God's peace offered by His Son, Jesus Christ.

Real peace is the peace of God.

> Be anxious for nothing, but in everything by prayer and supplication, with thanksgiving, let your requests be made know to God; and the peace of God, which surpasses all understanding, will guard your hearts and minds through Christ Jesus. (Philippians 4:6–7 NKJV)

tb Dusty Bible?

Satan is not afraid of a dusty Bible. He knows that if your Bible is dusty, you haven't been using it. And if you're not using it, it's just a matter of time before he can trick you by twisting God's Word. If you aren't reading God's Word every day, Satan may know God's Word better than you do.

Don't believe that Satan knows scripture? Read this.

> Then Jesus was led up by the Spirit into the wilderness to be tempted by the devil. And when He had fasted forty days and forty nights, afterward He was hungry.
>
> Now when the tempter came to Him, he said, "If You are the Son of God, command that these stones become bread."
>
> But He answered and said, "It is written: 'Man shall not live by bread alone, but by every word that proceeds from the mouth of God.'"
>
> Then the devil took Him up into the holy city; set Him on the pinnacle of the temple, and said to Him, "If You are the Son of God, throw Yourself down. For it is written: 'He shall give His angels charge over you.' and 'In their hands they shall bear you up, lest you dash your foot against a stone.'"
> (Matthew 4:1–6 NKJV)

Yeppers! When Satan said, "For it is written: 'He shall give His angels charge over you and in their hands they shall bear you up,'" Satan was quoting Psalm 91:11–12.

> For He shall give His angels charge over you, and to keep you in all your ways. In their hands they shall bear you up, lest you dash your foot against a stone. (Psalm 91:11–12 NKJV)

A wise man once told me that a worn and tattered Bible is the sign of a strong spiritual warrior. The Bible is a war manual for warriors. They need to know God's Word intimately before they go into battle. Satan will twist God's Word this way and that and use half-truths to suit his needs and trick us into believing in his ways instead of God's.

The book of Genesis shows us how Satan works. He twisted God's verbal word when he was talking with Eve in the garden. If he is bold enough to twist God's verbal words with someone who has walked and talked with God, he's bold enough to twist God's written Word with you.

How is your Bible? Is the cover looking well used? Are the pages earmarked? Does the binder show lots of use? Or is there a layer of dust on it? Will you have to blow it off before you can use it?

Will your Bible cause Satan to tremble? Or will it invite him in?

tb Hard to Sacrifice

John 3:16–17 tells us that God so loved the world that He gave His only Son so no one would perish, so all could spend eternity with Him in heaven if they choose. Wow!

So why do I find it hard when God asks me to sacrifice for Him? Why do I moan and groan when things get just a tad bit uncomfortable? Just how uncomfortable could I be when I'm not physically nailed to a cross or not having to give up my only son?

Why do I complain when things don't go as I have planned? When God changes my plans? Why must I act like a spoiled child when God implements His plans in place of mine? Who am I to question God?

When I accepted Jesus as my Savior, I accepted Him as my Lord. In John 10:30, Jesus told us that He and the heavenly Father, God, were one. So, when I accepted Jesus as my Lord, I also accepted God as my Lord.

And as my Lord, God has the right to tell me what to do and expect me to be obedient in doing it without any backtalk. These are the rights of a lord, the spiritual Lord or otherwise.

At times, being obedient to the Lord may mean I must sacrifice what I want to do to fulfill God's plans for me. I may have to give up what I want for what God wants me to have. Sounds one-sided, doesn't it?

But please remember that the second I accepted Jesus as my Savior, I accepted God as my Lord, and I did so with my free will. So God has the right to expect me to forfeit my plans for His.

Oddly, I have found that if I am obedient to God's plans, life is pleasant—exciting actually. And I am doing things I never thought I would. This book is only one example of how God's plans for your life can take you to places you never dreamed of going. God does not expect you to do what He asks you to do in your own strength; He will equip you with the gifts you need to accomplish His task for you and will provide a way for it to be done.

God does not call the qualified. He qualifies the called.

> Now may the God of peace who brought up our Lord Jesus from the dead, that great Shepherd of the sheep, through the blood of the everlasting covenant, make you complete in every good work to do His will, working in you what is well pleasing

in His sight, through Jesus Christ, to whom be glory forever and ever. Amen. (Hebrews 13:20–21 NKJV)

tb Food for Thought

Then the Angel of the LORD called to Abraham a second time out of heaven, and said, "By Myself I have sworn says the LORD, because you have done this thing; and have not withheld your son, your only son." (Genesis 22:15–16 NKJV)

After Abraham obeyed the Lord and offered his only son, Isaac, to be sacrificed, the Lord swore by Himself. Whom else could God swear by? There is no other like Him. God is great, strong, smart, and all knowing.

God is God. He is the commander's Commander. The highest of all authority. The power of the powerful. The wisdom of the wise. The righteousness of the righteous. The Almighty. The Creator of all. There is no one like Him!

So who else does God have to swear by but Himself?

tb Proverbs 8

Proverbs 8 is a book on great wisdom, one of the books in the Bible well worth studying.

Here are just some of the things we can learn from Proverbs 8.

1. Wisdom is truthful.

2. Wisdom is worthy.
3. Wisdom calls out to us.
4. Wisdom seeks us.
5. Wisdom is costly.
6. Wisdom is valuable.
7. Wisdom dwells among the prudent.
8. Wisdom gives understanding.

Proverbs 8 tells us that wisdom is honest, good, and worth having and that wisdom beckons us. We are told that wisdom will cost us something be it time, friends, or whatever. But no matter the cost, this wisdom is well worth the sacrifice because it will give us understanding and help make us caring and wise.

I can see something else in these verses. Or should I say someone else. Look again.

> Wisdom is truth, worthy, calls to us, seeks us, is costly, valuable, is found among the prudent, and gives us understanding.

Whom do you think these verses are talking about? Can you not see Jesus there? He is all these things—worthy, truthful, valuable, and costly—and He wants to be with us.

> Hear my instruction and be wise, and do not disdain it. Blessed is the man who listens to me, watching daily at my gates, waiting at the posts of my doors.

For whoever finds me finds life, and obtains favor from the LORD; but he who sins against me wrongs his own soul; and those who hate me love death. (Proverbs 8:33–36 NKJV)

tb Is Something Missing?

Good morning, Lord! I have so much to do today. To make sure I've done everything, let me go down my list. Let's see. I've made the bed, cooked breakfast, got hubby off to work, and fed the cats, horses, and dogs. Did the morning dishes and swept the kitchen. Watered the inside plants.

Hmmm.

Lord, I feel I left something out. Could You tell me what it is?

Does anyone see Bible reading, prayer time, or any time spent alone with God listed above? I think maybe that's what's missing. What do you think?

tb Why Should We Pay Taxes?

Tax season is here. *Arrg!* It seems we work hard all year to support our federal government, doesn't it? And we're not always happy with the way the government spends our money. We may find it easy to fluff the numbers just a bit on our tax returns. You know what I'm talking about—a tweak here and a twank there.

Or how about that large purchase with which we were able to bypass local sales taxes? Feeling pretty smug about that, aren't we?

Let me ask you as one Christian to another, why should we pay taxes? Outside the fact that possible jail time doesn't rate as your dream vacation. Or we wish to avoid IRS tax seizures of our assets. Why should we pay taxes?

Jesus told us to pay Caesar what belongs to Caesar. If you need a refresher, read Matthew 22:15–22 and

Mark 12:13–17. But there's another reason. It's found in Romans 13.

> Let every soul be subject to the governing authorities. For there is no authority except from God, and the authorities that exist are appointed by God. Therefore whoever resists the authority resists the ordinance of God, and those who resist will bring judgment on themselves.
>
> For rulers are not a terror to good works, but to evil. Do you want to be unafraid of the authority? Do what is good, and you will have praise from the same. For he is God's minister to you for good. But if you do evil, be afraid; for he does not bear the sword in vain; for he is God's minister, an avenger to execute wrath on him who practices evil. Therefore you must be subject not only because of wrath but also for conscience' sake.
>
> For because of this you also pay taxes, for they are God's ministers attending continually to this very thing. Render therefore to all their due: taxes to whom taxes are due, customs to whom customs, fear to whom fear, honor to whom honor. Owe no one anything except to love one another, for he who loves another has fulfilled the law. (Romans 13:1–8 NKJV)

So why do we pay our taxes—local, state, and federal? According to what we have just read, those who are in government offices are there because God wants them there. They're doing work for God even if it's without their knowledge. And our taxes help finance that work.

We Christians are to be honest and of great integrity, which means no lying on any form whether hedging on numbers or underreporting. Romans tells us that to do so is evil and dangerous. God's minister is an avenger who will execute wrath on those who practice evil.

And as if that weren't bad enough, whoever rebels against what God has instituted will bring judgment on themselves. Scary!

So why should I pay all my taxes? Because God said to.

tb Which Sign Are You?

There has been a lot of talk on the news about astrological signs. It appears as if these signs are not correct due to the tilting of the earth's axis. This has caused a great deal of havoc and concern. People do not know just which sign they were really born under. And unless this information is correct, people will not know how their day or their lives will go for they will be reading the wrong sign. That information found under the wrong sign will be for someone else.

How sad. All this foretelling of one's future is another one of Satan's lies, but people still listen.

Aren't you glad you don't have to worry about such things? Aren't you glad your life lies in the hands of the One who set you free of worry about the future? Free to live your life fully and with zest regardless of which month you were born in?

We can rest assured that no matter what happens to

us, we are in the hands of a God who loves us greatly and who can and will take care of us. What a great place to be!

By the way, this is my sign. ✚

tb Trust in the Lord

I have been recovering from a broken leg, multiple bone surgeries, and complications of infection. My life for the past six months has consisted of doctor visits, physical therapy, trips to the drugstore, home health care visits, IV therapy, and an endless stream of wound care. Not much more. But finally, the wound seems to be almost healed.

Filled with hope and praise for Jesus, I checked the mailbox and found a $10 check from a medical bill I had overpaid. "Wow! Thank You, Jesus. You are awesome!" I said with thankfulness. I put the check in my purse and went on with my day.

The next morning while I was in the shower, my wound broke open and started draining again. Oh really? *Arrg!* Since it was Saturday, I had to leave messages with the answering services of both physicians. Returning my call, they gave me instructions for the weekend and told me to be at the surgeon's office Monday morning for cultures— again. Filled with discouragement, I turned to the Lord and instead of saying, "Wow, God, You are awesome!" all I could muster was a rather flat "Oh really, Lord?" complete with a deep sigh of defeat.

Monday morning found us at the surgeon's office. The physician's assistant collected a culture specimen and opened and drained my wound. Again, instead of praising God, all I could muster was a deep sigh.

My surgeon said I should come back on Friday for the results of the culture and told me to have a good day. Instead of praising God, all I could do was sigh.

My next stop was the checkout window, and our copay for that visit was $10.44. Remember that $10 check? The Lord knew that I would be at the doctor's office on Monday and that I would need that money.

But that's not all.

When I checked the mailbox on the way home from the doctor's office, I found another check to cover an overpayment in the amount of 45¢. Yes, someone had sent me a 45¢ check!

God gave me enough to pay that $10.44 with change left over. Now you tell me—is God awesome or what?

tb The Power of a Godly Wife

> Wives, likewise, be submissive to your own husbands, that even if some do not obey the word, they, without a word, may be won by the conduct of their wives, when they observe your chaste conduct accompanied by fear. (1 Peter 3:1–2 NKJV)

By living a godly life with gentleness and a quiet spirit, a wife can deliver a powerful sermon to her husband without saying a word. I recently heard a saying that is most fitting here: Be sure to preach the gospel to everyone you come in contact with. And use words if necessary.

Ladies, that includes our husbands.

tb Proverbs 25:28

> Like a city whose walls are broken down
> is a man who lacks self-control. (Proverbs
> 25:28 NIV)

In biblical times, cities were surrounded by walls for protection from enemies. If walls were broken, enemies could easily enter the city and take control of it.

Those who cannot or will not rule over their spirits are without self-control and self-discipline. They are like cities with broken walls that Satan can easily conquer.

Without good, strong walls, Satan can move right in and take control of them. We are told this in Ephesians 6:10–18.

> Be self-controlled and alert. Your enemy the
> devil prowls around like a roaring lion looking
> for someone to devour. (1 Peter 5:8 NIV)

Satan is looking for those whose walls are broken so he may conquer and devour them.

We must have self-control, self-discipline in all areas of our lives—finances, time management, relationships, communication, and even hobbies.

We are to rule over our spirits everywhere we go—on the job, off the job, at the grocery store, gas station, fast-food restaurant, and even in church.

In doing so, we will keep our walls strong and in good repair and will be great representatives of our Lord and Savior, Jesus.

Now that's what I call a win-win!

tb *Then* I Will Hear from Heaven

> When I shut up heaven and there is no rain, or command the locusts to devour the land, or send pestilence among My people, if My people who are called by My name will humble themselves, and pray and seek My face, and turn from their wicked ways, then I will hear from heaven, and will forgive their sin and heal their land. (2 Chronicles 7:13–14 NKJV)

What power is found in this scripture! What a wonderful promise from God. But if you look closely, you will see a few things we must do, a few things God has asked of us so He can keep His promise.

First off, let us look at the fact that God did not say "if I" or "should I"; He said, "when I." Which means these things will happen in some form be it a drought of nature or a drought of _____. You fill in the blank.

And when these things happen, God has said that if His people do a few things He has asked of them, He would keep His promise. *If* is the most powerful two-letter word found in our language. *If* I had only done this. *If* only I had not done that. *If* only I had listened.

God tells us here that if we, His people, do some things, He will turn His attention to us, hear our prayers, and answer them.

So what has God asked His people to do?

1. Humble themselves before Him.
2. Pray to Him.

3. Seek Him.
4. Turn from their wicked ways.

God promised that if we do these things, He will hear from heaven, forgive our sins, and heal our land. God promised that if we humble ourselves before Him, He will answer our prayers.

What a wonderful God we serve! He warns us of upcoming droughts and plagues and tells us what to do when we're in them! He gives us a list of things that will unlock His floodgates of blessings.

And then He blesses us.

tb Evil vs. Good

Satan tries to use certain things for evil that God uses for good. Here are some examples.

In Matthew 4:1–11, the devil tempted Jesus three times in many areas of life. The devil was searching for Jesus's Achilles' heel. Instead of causing Jesus to fall into sin, Satan's temptations proved Jesus was sinless.

Exodus 13:17–14:31 gives us a look at Moses and the nation of Israel placed between the Red Sea and bloodthirsty Egyptians. What a victory that could have been for Satan—wiping out the entire nation of Israel at one time. But God gave His people a clear, dry path across the Red Sea and drowned their approaching enemy.

In Acts 7:54–8:1, we see Stephen, a great man of God, being stoned for sharing God's Word. As Stephen was dying, he gave those around him, even those who were stoning him, an eyewitness report of the heavens opening and of seeing Jesus standing at the right hand of the heavenly Father. After such an experience, how could they not believe? Even those who did not want to believe had no choice but to believe what they had just heard. God gave them a glimpse of His glory by the lips of a dying man.

My favorite one is when Judas betrayed Jesus.

> And the chief priests and the scribes sought how they might kill Him, for they feared the people. Then Satan entered Judas, surnamed Iscariot, who was numbered among the twelve. So he went his way and conferred with the chief priests and captains, how he might betray Him to them.

> And they were glad, and agreed to give him money. So he promised and sought opportunity to betray Him to them in the absence of the multitude. (Luke 22:2–6 NKJV)

How Satan and his angels must have hooted, danced, and celebrated over Judas's act! Over what they thought was one of Satan's greatest accomplishments. One of the twelve disciples, one of Jesus's most intimate followers, had just sold Him out. I am sure Satan and his demons put on one good party.

But unknown to Satan—for he is not all knowing as God is—this act was the beginning of humanity's salvation. By telling the chief priests and teachers where they could find Jesus, Judas set in motion a string of events—God's plan to provide you and me with the powerful, saving grace we enjoy today. Because Satan entered Judas and caused him to betray Jesus, we are now covered in Jesus's life-giving blood for eternity.

Unbeknownst to Satan, Jesus's betrayal is my lifeline. So once again, God wins.

tb James

> My brethren, count it all joy when you fall into various trials, knowing that the testing of your faith produces patience.
>
> But let patience have its perfect work, that you may be perfect and complete, lacking nothing. (James 1:2–4 NKJV)

We often think of the trials God allows in our lives as tests. We often say, "God is testing me." And maybe He is.

But in reality, these tests are not for God. He already knows our strengths and weaknesses. These tests are for us, and they are necessary; they show us our strengths and weaknesses and can even be wake-up calls if our hearts aren't in the right place.

Trials also allow us to see just how God can and will work in our lives. We usually will not see God's hand working unless we look for it. There must be a reason that makes us turn to God with humble hearts. So unless we are in the pressure cooker, we may never learn to be aware of God and His ways.

Trials can be times of deep walks with our Lord. They tend to make us turn to Him for what we need. They cause us to seek Him for comfort and guidance. They are times of God's provision and protection.

As we strain under the heavy load of our trials, we experience God's mercy in a different way, a way that is much more personal and real. Our trials seem to create in us a sensitivity for God and the things of God. They remove the scales from our eyes, the plugs from our ears, and the calluses from our hearts.

We know our Lord loves us very much and takes care of His own. But our trials will take that knowledge from our brains and place it in our hearts. Our trials will help us believe Jesus when He tells us He will be closer to us than a brother. Our trials will help us grow into mature Christians.

Yes, trials are hard, and I don't like them any more than you do, but don't waste your trials because they are strong fertilizer for your faith. Use them to grow the faith and wisdom areas of your spiritual walk. Let them draw you closer to God. Let them show you how God can work in your life.

And that He will!

tb Happy Holiday!

This world has followed Satan's gentle yet persuasive lead away from the good things of God to the things of a perverted lifestyle. Take Christmas for example. This holiday has become a competitive sport between those who say "Happy Holiday" and those who say "Merry Christmas." It has become a time of boycotting stores that sell "holiday" trees and supporting those that sell "Christmas" trees. And vice versa. As if there's a difference?

But I googled the word *holiday* and found that it comes from the Old English word *Haligdaeg*, which means "Holy Day." Those who refuse to say "Merry Christmas" because "Christ" is in the word and say "Happy Holiday" instead are actually saying "Happy Holy Day." While they think they are protesting the religious part of Christmas, they are actually supporting it. They just don't know it. Now ain't that a hoot?

And then there is all the me-ism that occurs during this time of the year. It's all about what I want, when I want it, and how I can get it. This time of the year seems to have turned into a self-centered, me-first buying frenzy that is far greater than any great white shark episode.

If Satan can keep us running around looking for just the right gift or worrying about how decorated our houses are, we may lose sight of why we bought the gift or why we decorated our homes. If Satan can keep us struggling with an over-obligated schedule of cooking and parties and plays, we may be too busy to have time for celebrating the real reason for Christmas, the birth of Jesus.

And if Jesus has been squeezed out of Christmas, Satan has succeeded in making Christmas about everything but what it really is supposed to be. Satan has been able to turn this most wonderful time of the year—the time we Christians celebrate the birth of our Lord and Savior, Jesus Christ—into something that reeks of greed and selfishness.

However, no matter how hard Satan tries to cover up the real reason for Christmas, this holiday is still *Christ*mas because Jesus still reigns; He always has and always will.

tb Breathe

This morning as I brushed my teeth and did all the usual morning preps for the day, my dog Levi was lying just outside the bathroom door. He was very quiet and quite content as he watched me go about my morning routine.

When I walked to the door to leave, Levi did not move. Instead, he sat up and looked me square in the eye asking for my affection. So I kissed him on his head.

Then Levi did the oddest thing—he stuck his nose close to my mouth and breathed in my breath. He inhaled long and strong. It was as if he were trying to breathe me into himself, as if he wanted to take in all of me he could. What a humbling and yet uplifting moment! There was is a dog I loved dearly showing me he loved me so much that he wanted a part of me to be a part of him.

And then I thought about God. About how He would feel if I placed my nose close to His mouth and breathed in His breath. If I inhaled Him long and strong right into my being.

What a great expression of love that would be. How uplifting it would be to God if I showed such desire to have Him be a part of me that I would breathe Him in so hard that He became part of me.

I know that God breathes us; He told us that we were as the sweet aroma of Christ in His nostrils. God has told us that we, those who are saved by the blood of Jesus, are sweet smelling to Him while those who are not saved smell of death.

> Now thanks be to God who always leads us in triumph in Christ, and through us diffuses the fragrance of His Knowledge in every place.

> For we are to God the fragrance of Christ among those who are being saved and among those who are perishing.

To the one we are the aroma of death leading to death, and to the other the aroma of life leading to life.

And who is sufficient for these things? (2 Corinthians 2:14–16 NKJV)

The NIV says, "to God we are the aroma of Christ." Wow. The aroma of Jesus Christ Himself!

Are you breathing in God? Are you showing Him that your love for Him is so great that you want Him to be part of you? When you take in great big breaths, are you breathing in all of God you can?

tb Sometimes God Says No

Jesus prayed in the garden asking God to take away the hardship He was about to endure. Jesus pleaded with God, His Father, to not ask Him to walk the painful path laid out before Him. He asked God to allow Him to walk a different path.

But God said no; He asked Jesus to walk the path laden with pain so humanity could have salvation. Unless Jesus went to the cross as our sacrificial sin Lamb, there would be no blood sacrifice and thus no salvation for sinners.

How did Jesus respond to God's no? Did He pout? Threaten to walk away from God? Refuse to do as God had asked Him to do? Did He tell God, "If you love me, you will not ask Me to do this"? Did He try to bargain with God?

No.

Jesus accepted His assignment from God. And He

prayed for His disciples and for all His future followers asking God to take care of them.

> Now I am no longer in the world, but these are in the world, and I come to You. Holy Father, keep through Your name those whom You have given Me, that they may be one as We are. (John 17:11 NKJV)

And then He died.

tb The Ice Cube Dog

Due to a serious injury, my last two years have included numerous hours with an ice bag. When Levi, my dog, hears me rumbling around in the ice tray for cubes, he comes running, sits down facing me, and asks with his big, brown eyes for an ice cube. He will always sit in the same place in the same way and face me. He will wait patiently for his ice cube because he has faith that when he asks, I will give.

And I do. But I give only when he asks. Should he be in his crate dog napping, (he can't be catnapping because he's not a cat), I don't wake him and ask if he'd like an ice cube. I give him one only when he's sitting in front of me asking for one.

But I do give him an ice cube every time he asks for one; I don't shortchange him.

We can learn a very valuable lesson from Levi's actions. Jesus told us that if we go to Him, we will receive. If we wait on Him patiently just as Levi does for his ice cubes, we will receive what we have asked for.

Ask and it will be given to you; seek and you
will find; knock and it will be opened to you.
For everyone who asks receives, and he who
seeks finds, and to him who knocks it will be
opened. (Matthew 7:7–8 NKJV)

When we ask Jesus for an ice cube and patiently wait
for one, we will receive one every time. Because Jesus will
not shortchange us.

tb Dogged Obedience

My husband and I were carving a ham while our eighty-
pound dog mingled among us. His head was almost tall
enough to reach the kitchen counter on which we were
working. After a few minutes, the dog lost interest and lay
down on the floor a few feet away.

We cut up the ham, put it in bags, and froze it. I found a
small piece left on the plate. Wanting to reward my dog for
his good behavior, I called his name. He promptly jumped
up, rushed to me, and sat when I asked him to. I gave him
his reward; I was pleased with his obedient behavior.

I was pleased with his obedient behavior.

Hmmm.

If I were as obedient to the Lord as my dog is to me, I
would run right over and do whatever He asked me to do
when He asked. And I would do so with great anticipation
and willingness.

I would be willing to do whatever the Lord asked me
to do the minute He asked it in haste and with vigor and
eagerness. Most importantly, I would do it with a willing
heart, a heart that wanted to please God. A heart that

wanted to hear God say, "Well done My good and faithful servant."

What is my reward for such obedience? I can tell you, it's much better than a piece of ham.

If you are willing and obedient, you will eat the good of the land. (Isaiah 1:19 NKJV)

tb Tithing and Thanksgiving

Tithing and Thanksgiving may not seem to be on the same plane, but they are.

Tithing has always been equated with giving, but God views it as an act of worship, of thanksgiving. Our finances—our tithes and offerings—can directly influence God's blessings. Only when we are faithful in our financial giving can God give so much more back to us.

God is always faithful to us; He loves us very much and wants only the best for us. And He wants to bless our socks off! But His blessings are not always cold, hard cash. His blessings can be the clothes someone gives us. Or a ride to the store when our cars are in the shop. And what about that wonderful dinner someone gave you when you were ill? Or the phone call we received when we were feeling down and out? Those are God's blessings too.

God uses others to bless His children. And when He does, it is the one time when being used feels good to the one who is being used. When you do such things for others, you allow God to shower them with blessings and love through you.

When we are faithful and steady in our financial support of God's church and His ministries, we are showing God we have finally understood our money is from Him alone, not our abilities.

Yes, I know, your paychecks come from your employer. But didn't God give you that job and the ability to do it? Ultimately, your paycheck does not come from you or from your employer, but from God.

This means that tithing, giving 10 percent of your finances to God, is a form of worship, a way of thanking God for giving it to you in the first place.

Tithing and thanksgiving go hand in hand. How can you tithe without having something to tithe from? How can you not be thankful to a God who provides you with something to tithe with?

Tithing is one place we can influence God's blessings for this reason.

> "Will a man rob God? You have robbed Me! But you say, 'In what way have we robbed You?' In tithes and offerings."

> "You are cursed with a curse, for you have robbed Me, even this whole nation. Bring all the tithes into the storehouse, that there may be food in My house, and try Me now in this," says the LORD of hosts, "If I will not open for you the windows of heaven and pour out for you such blessing that there will not be room enough to receive it." (Malachi 3:8–10 NKJV)

tb Helping God

I tend to help God. Imagine such a thing. Me helping God. But yes sir! There I am! Me in all my human wisdom! Helping the One who created the universe! As if He needs my help!

Come on! How could I possibly think God needs me to help Him with anything? How could I think I know how to do things better than God does, better than the One who created the earth just by speaking? Better than He who made all the universe and hung each star and planet just where it should be? Better than the One who created me? And with His breath blew life into my lungs?

Oh really? Imagine that!

But as I laugh at such a silly notion, I wonder why I feel the need to help God. Could it be that I don't trust God 100 percent of the time with all the things in my life?

Could it be I don't trust the way God will handle things? Could it be that after all the times He has protected and provided for me, I still doubt He will work things out with my best interests in mind? That I still, have an issue of trust, with God?

If I am dealing with trusting God or rather with not trusting Him, where is my faith? This is a very serious issue because God's Word tells us that unless we have faith, we cannot please Him.

> But without faith it is impossible to please Him, for he who comes to God must believe that He is, and that He is a rewarder of those who diligently seek Him. (Hebrews 11:6 NKJV)

Or instead of a lack of faith, could my need to help God be a form of that dreaded five-letter word *pride?*

Eeek!

Pride is not good. God does not like pride. He doesn't mess around when it comes to pride and prideful situations. Just ask Satan.

> How you have fallen from heaven O morning star, son of the dawn! You have been cast down to the earth, you who once laid low the nations! You said in your heart, "I will ascend to heaven; I will raise my throne above the stars of God; I will sit enthroned on the mount of assembly, on the utmost heights of the sacred mountain. I will ascend above the tops of the clouds; I will make myself like the Most High."

> But you are brought down to the grave, to the depths of the pit. (Isaiah 14:12–15 NIV)

Satan was so filled with pride that he not only wanted God's place in heaven, he also wanted to sit on God's throne. Satan is still extremely prideful; just look at the behavior of his children.

But let us also look at what happened to that prideful Satan! First, he was kicked out of heaven.

> And war broke out in heaven; Michael and his angels fought with the dragon; and the dragon and his angels fought, but they did not prevail, nor was a place found for them in heaven any longer.

> So the great dragon was cast out, that serpent of old, called the Devil and Satan, who deceives the whole world; he was cast to the earth, and his angels were cast out with him. (Revelation 12:7–9 NKJV)

And then he was cast into hell for eternity.

> The devil who deceived them, was cast into the lake of fire and brimstone where the beast and the false prophet are. And they will be tormented day and night forever and ever. (Revelation 20:10 NKJV)

This is one of the few times we can actually learn from Satan. Yes, that's right! When we read what God has planned for him, we learn a great lesson—pride separates us from God for eternity and can kill us.

Regardless of the reason for wanting to help God, we all must learn to wait on Him and do things His way, not ours, and in His time, not ours. For me, that will be a lifelong lesson.

tb They Cannot Understand

We should not be surprised when those who are not Christians cannot understand what we try to tell them about Jesus and God. We are told that those who are not of God cannot understand the things of God. We are told that they find the things of God as foolishness.

But the natural man does not receive the things of the Spirit of God, for they are foolishness to him; nor can he know them, because they are spiritually discerned. (1 Corinthians 2:14 NKJV)

In every aspect of life, you will find lingo attached to it. Doctors use medical words, mechanics use car words, and attorneys use legal words. The same is true for those who study scripture.

Some of this lingo may be applied to the above scripture, but I wonder if the scripture doesn't go deeper. If you're not a child of God, you're a child of Satan; there's no third person; no third choice; no fence to sit on. God or Satan period.

Those who have not accepted Jesus Christ as their personal Lord and Savior have by default accepted Satan as their lord. Sadly, most who are following Satan don't know it. They think they're living life their way when in reality they're living life Satan's way. If you were to tell them they were children of Satan, they would get angry with you because no one really wants to be one of Satan's children.

But ironically, since they are not God's children, they cannot understand what you try to tell them when you speak of God and of His ways, because they are of Satan, not of God. Those who aren't of God cannot understand the things of God.

It is as if Satan has his fingers stuck in their ears to keep them from hearing God's Word be it accidentally or intentionally. Satan knows the minute they hear and understand God's Word, their spiritual eyes will open and they will no longer be his children and no longer do his work. They will be doing the work of Jesus and of God. The last thing Satan wants is another Christian telling others about the cleansing blood of Jesus, about how much God loves them, and about how God wants them to be His.

Satan knows that when someone hears about God's Word and believes in the cleansing blood of Jesus, he loses a warrior. And if he loses enough warriors, he will lose the spiritual battle. So he lies and deceives in hopes of keeping his warriors and maybe even gaining a few new ones.

But sorry, Satan! You need to read Revelation! Oh yeah, I forgot. Maybe you don't have a Bible. Well, let me tell you what Revelation says.

You lose!

tb Free Indeed

Leviticus 1–7 gives instructions on how God wanted His sacrifices to be performed. There were at least six sacrifices or offerings as they are called in the NKJV, seven if you count the offering for the unintentional sin. Yep, there's an offering for the sin we accidentally commit.

God laid out details on how He wanted the sacrifices to be handled. In some sacrifices, the entire offering was to be burned. In others, the kidneys and fatty areas were not. In another, the hide was to be kept from the fire. Some of the offerings were to come from herds and some from flocks. And then there was the grain offering, the wave offering, and two others God called the most holy of offerings—the sin offering and the trespass offering.

Whew! The priests of Old Testament times were busy.

But Jesus put a stop to all that; He was the Sacrifice to

end all sacrifices. Jesus was our personal sin and trespass offering rolled up in one and the only Sacrifice needed to fulfill all the other offerings. He is the Sacrifice for all who accept Him as their Savior—everyone who has lived, is living, and will live. He is their personal sin and trespass offering for eternity.

By dying on the cross, Jesus freed us from having to perform all the offerings or sacrifices we read about in Leviticus. We no longer have to worry about sacrificing for our accidental or not-so-accidental sins. We no longer have to concern ourselves with the grain offering, the fellowship offering, or the burnt offering. We have been freed from such things. Jesus's blood has freed us from trying to follow all these sacrificial laws.

When we realize this, we will have a new understanding of what Jesus was telling us when He said,

> Most assuredly, I say to you, whoever commits sin is a slave to sin. And a slave does not abide in the house forever, but a son abides forever. Therefore if the Son makes you free, you shall be free indeed. (John 8:34–36 NKJV)

Our sacrifices have been paid in full by the King of Kings and the Lord of Lords. How good is that?

tb Roses

I love roses. They are the prettiest flower God has given us. When I needed to create some privacy, I chose four climbing roses that live on a trellis just outside my bathroom. Once they are tall enough, I will see them through my bathroom window. How lovely.

I planted two of the four roses. Not being sure where to plant the others, I left them in their pots next to the two I had planted.

After a short time, I noticed a difference in the four plants. The two in pots were not quite as healthy as the two in the ground.

All four plants had received the same amount of fertilizer, sun, and water, but the two in the pots seemed to be dying while the two in the ground were doing well and actually producing roses.

Hmmm. This is a lot like Christians. The roses in the pots are like Christians who are planted in the world. While the roses planted in the ground are like Christians planted in God's Word.

The Christians planted in God's Word are doing well while the Christians planted in the world seem to be wilting. They are all receiving the same sermons, Bible studies, and times of fellowship, but the Christians planted in the world are struggling to stay alive while the Christians planted in the Word are flourishing.

As it is with the roses, both groups appear to be Christians, but only the group planted in God's Word is blooming with the fruits of the Spirit.

So, let me ask you. Which rose are you? Are you planted in the world like the roses in the pots or in the Word like the roses in the ground?

> I am the vine, you are the branches. He who abides in Me, and I in him, bears much fruit; for without Me you can do nothing. (John 15:5 NKJV)

tb The Man from Nowhere

A man walked into our service and sat in the back pew. He was someone we had not seen before. He appeared to be homeless.

After the service, he told us his name and that he had been saved in 1963 while in prison. He told us God had told him to go to churches and tell them that Christians needed to start standing up for God and being Christians; they needed to start telling everyone they saw about Jesus Christ because He was coming back very soon.

He said America was doomed to hell if the church didn't start being the church and worshipping God as the church was supposed to.

He said God was giving America and its churches one more chance. God had told him to go to all the churches and tell them these things.

When I first saw the man, I thought he was just a homeless man looking for some food or maybe a few dollars. Yes, to my shame, I thought he was just wanting something from us as a church.

I know churches are to minister to those in need, but some think that churches owe them something and should give them what they want. They are not really interested in hearing about Jesus. They don't really care if Jesus wants to be their Savior or that God is the God of all creation. No. They look at churches as places to scavenge.

But after listening to him, I was not so sure. I wondered if this man was truly a messenger from God or just a broken man who was rambling. A man who just wanted to sit in air conditioning and catch a good sermon. A man who was repeating something he has heard.

I wonder.

Is this how the Pharisees felt when Jesus showed up at their synagogues teaching everyone who would listen to Him? Did they wonder if Jesus was just a homeless man who was rambling? Did they wonder if He was there to steal their thunder? To stir up trouble? We are told that Jesus spoke God's Word with the power of the Holy Spirit and the people praised Him.

> Then Jesus returned in the power of the Spirit to Galilee, and news of Him went out through all the surrounding region. And He taught in their synagogues, being glorified by all. (Luke 4:14–15 NKJV)

Either way, my church welcomed this man, fed him, and sent him on his way with food and water. We made sure he felt loved and cared for. Isn't that what Jesus taught us? To love our neighbors and to minister to their needs? Whether they are homeless people who are just rambling or are truly people delivering a word from God?

In doing so, we may unknowingly minister to one of God's messengers. Or maybe even an angel!

> Do not forget to entertain strangers, for by so doing some have unwittingly entertained angels. (Hebrews 13:2 NKJV)

tb This Little Light of Mine

This little light of mine, I'm gonna let it shine.
This little light of mine, I'm gonna let it shine.
This little light of mine, I'm gonna let it shine.
Let it shine. Let it shine. Let it shine.
Hmmm. Got that covered.
Won't let Satan blow it out. No! I'm gonna let it shine.
Won't let Satan blow it out. No! I'm gonna let it shine.
Won't let Satan blow it out. No! I'm gonna let it shine.
Let it shine. Let it shine. Let it shine.
Yep. Good here too.
Won't hide it under a bushel. No! I'm gonna let it shine.
Won't hide it under a bushel. No! I'm gonna let it shine.
Won't hide it under a bushel. No!
I'm gonna let it shine.
Let it shine. Let it shine. Let it shine.
Ooops!
I might have a problem here! Just where is my little light? Am I holding it up for all the world to see or just for my part of the world?

Am I giving light to everyone in the house or just to those in one room?

Am I living a life that causes others to see my little light shining brightly, or do I allow life's trials to obscure its glow?

Am I placing my lit candle on the tallest candle stand so everyone can see it? Or have I placed it on a stand that is too short for anyone to see?

And to those who do not have this little light to share, why not? If it is because they don't know Jesus, I want to introduce Him to them.

"May I present to you Jesus Christ, God's only Son, who willingly laid His life down for you as your personal sacrificial sin Lamb so you can talk with, walk with, and eventually live with God for eternity.

"Jesus is also your great Shepherd. He loves you very deeply and wants to live your life with you. Please accept Him today by acknowledging that He is indeed the Son of God who died on the cross for your sins and was resurrected in three days. That He is the only way to God's mansion, heaven. Allow Him to take His place on the throne of your hearts."

And for those of you who know who Jesus is—turn your lights on! We live in a dark world filled with the things of darkness. We live in a world that needs light and the things of light. Jesus told us we were supposed to be a light, His light.

> You are the light of the world. A city that is set on a hill cannot be hidden. Nor do they light a lamp and put it under a basket, but on a lampstand, and it gives light to all who are in the house. Let your light so shine before men, that they may see your good works and glorify your Father in heaven. (Matthew 5:14–16 NKJV)

tb Regular Maintenance

One of the great things about living in the country is that you don't have to pay for water or sewer. You get water from a well, and your sewage goes into a septic tank and then into a drain field. This setup is very efficient and saves you hundreds of dollars.

You do, however, need to maintain these two systems. The filtering system on the pump needs to be kept clean and the holding tank's pressure kept at just the right settings. The septic tank needs to be pumped out from time to time, and there is no driving anything bigger than my John Deere in that part of the yard.

One Sunday morning, I put a load of clothes in the washing machine. I have worship services on Saturday nights, so no heathen here! All was well until the washer reached the spin cycle. The washing machine spun the water out of its tub and right into all the sinks, tubs, showers, and toilets. Yuck! Thank you, Lord, that it was water from only the washing machine and not … Well, you know.

My husband and I went outside and removed the cap from the septic tank nozzle; water spewed out giving us our own Old Faithful. From the looks of our geyser, the buildup in the tank must have been huge.

We called a septic tank company for an emergency pump. Arriving in a very timely manner, the septic tank man looked over our mess and concurred that the tank must have been very full.

He hooked up a large hose from his truck to our septic tank and scolded us for allowing the tank to go so long without maintenance. Feeling embarrassed, I listened and then left.

When I looked back I saw the man holding a large hose stuck down into a hole in my yard. The hose was sucking out something gross, smelly, and undesirable—life's manure.

But I also saw something else. I saw what happened when I first asked Jesus to save me. I saw Jesus sucking the awful, stinking mess that life can leave behind right out of my heart. Wow!

Everyone who is alive has had a life before accepting Jesus Christ as his or her Savior. Even those who were brought up in the church. Yeppers! Even them! I sometimes refer to this time as my BC time, my Before Christ time.

The lives we lived before allowing Jesus into our hearts are just like my septic tank full of life's gross, smelly, undesirable manure also known as sin. The longer we have lived that lifestyle, the one without Jesus in our BC times, the fuller our sin tanks will be.

Some of us have had sin tanks so full that the pressure inside could have caused an explosion. Others have had tanks that did explode or burst at the seams allowing that smelly, gross, undesirable sin to ooze out. Nonetheless, we all had some type of messy sin that only Jesus could pump out of our hearts.

And don't think that just because you're now one of God's children that your tank doesn't need regular maintenance, that your sin tank can't become overfilled with sin. Just like my septic tank needs regular maintenance, our hearts need regular maintenance.

Any septic tank company can handle a septic tank, but only Jesus can pump out your sin tank. You have to call Jesus to come and clean out life's manure—sin—from your heart regularly. If you don't, your sin will ooze out of your tank's busted seams or spew out as your own Old Faithful geyser of sin.

Guaranteed.

tb Black Spot

On a wonderful Florida afternoon, I was trimming my roses and clipping off the dead bark along with the leaves that had black spot. Black spot is a fungus usually found in areas not exposed to sunlight. So, most of the black spot leaves were smaller and younger and growing under larger leaves or clusters of leaves.

The lack of exposure to the sun allows the black spot fungus to prosper and spread. I know no other way of eradicating the fungus than to remove the part of the plant with the fungus.

Cutting off the young leaves infected with black spot allows sunshine to penetrate the cluster of leaves and prevent the spread and the return of the fungus. As much as you dislike removing young, tender leaves before they have a chance to mature, it must be done for the health of the plant itself.

As I was clipping off the leaves with black spot, this scripture about hidden sin came to mind.

> For nothing is secret that will not be revealed,
> nor anything hidden that will not be known
> and come to light. (Luke 8:17 NKJV)

Black spot is just like the sin in our lives. It penetrates areas where the Son does not. Or rather, it penetrates the areas we don't allow the Son to penetrate. Just as black spot will spread to other parts of the rose plant, our black spot sin will spread to the other parts of our lives. And sometimes, God may have to remove some of the young, tender parts of our lives to eradicate the sin that has penetrated that area.

Yes, this is usually painful. I think God dislikes having to trim off our areas infested with sin, but just as with the rose plant, He does so for His children' health and because He loves them.

Are there any leaves in your life that have black spot? Are there any hidden sin areas God will have to trim off? Are there any areas in your life that need exposure to the Son's light?

Yes? Then expose them to the Son. Doing so is the only way to keep sin eradicated.

tb Words Can Deeply Harm Us

Sticks and stones may break my bones, but words will never harm me. We've all heard that, but it's not quite true.

In fact, this statement verges on being a lie. According to scripture, this saying should really say, "Sticks and stones can break my bones and words will deeply harm me."

We all like to talk. And at times, we talk too much and say things that cut into a brother or sister like a sharp knife. Once our tongues deliver harmful words, those words are out there in the open floating around in space forever.

Words can be very harmful when we use them in unwise ways. When we engage our mouths before we engage our brains, we may say unthoughtful, unloving, or gossipy things. When we use words as weapons, they can deliver deep, painful, emotional wounds that may never heal. Or should they heal, they leave behind scars.

Therefore, we all need to take heed and choose our words very carefully before we speak.

Yes, sticks and stones may break our bones, but words can kill us.

> Death and life are in the power of the tongue, and those who love it will eat its fruit. (Proverbs 18:21 NKJV)

tb The Lord Giveth and Taketh Away

The Lord giveth and taketh away.

We usually hear those words at funerals as we mourn the loss of loved ones. However, this truth is found in all areas of our lives. Those of us who are aging faster than we wish to, can relate to this statement. Look at the changes in our health and our bodies. It seems as if God gave us strong, healthy bodies only to take them away as we age.

The Lord gives, and the Lord takes away not only in our physical areas but in other areas as well. When God opens doors for us, when He blesses us, we should grab those blessings! We should enjoy them. Give thanks to the Lord for them. Use them. But, do not hold onto them too tightly.

For when the Lord wants to give you new blessings, He may want to remove the old ones first. And if you are clutching your old blessings with a tight fist, God may have to pry your hand open to remove them and to give you the new ones. That can be painful. The harder you are clutching onto the old blessings, the harder God will have to pry. The harder God has to pry, the more intense the pain. Sometimes, the pain can be so great that it will cause you to take your eyes off your blessings. *Ouch!*

Yes, God gives and takes as He pleases. At times, you won't understand why He takes away certain things and not others or why He gives this and not that.

But God loves you very much. Though there are times when it doesn't seem so, He wants only the best for you, His child.

Do God and yourself a favor. Hold God's blessings with an open hand. Doing so will make it easier for God and less painful for you when He has to remove the old so to give you the new.

tb Not in the Name of Jesus Christ? Really?

When my pastor arrived for work one day, I followed him into his office and told him, "I have exciting news! The city called and asked if you would provide them with prayer at their business meeting next week. It will be on Thursday at seven p.m. This is a great opportunity to share our faith! Shall I call them and accept their invitation?"

My very wise pastor, tickled at my enthusiasm, looked over his glasses at me with a small grin and asked, "Will they allow me to pray in the name of Jesus?"

Taken aback by his question, I asked, "What do you mean?"

"If they will accept that I pray in the name of my Lord and Savior, Jesus Christ, I will be happy to provide them with an opening prayer. Otherwise, they need to find another minister," he said in a matter-of-fact tone.

Really? Do people pray to God without praying the name of His only Son? Do people approach the throne of God without the covering of Jesus's blood? Do they not know what they are doing?

The name of Jesus Christ is extremely powerful. Even Satan and his demons know the name of Jesus, and they tremble at His power.

> You believe that there is one God. You do well. Even the demons believe—and tremble. (James 2:19 NKJV)

The demons know the name of Jesus Christ and of His power; they must obey Him. The power of Jesus and His name is far greater than that of the demons and Satan.

> Now there was a man in their synagogue with an unclean spirit. And he cried out, saying, "Let us alone! What have we to do with You, Jesus of Nazareth? Did you come to destroy us? I know who You are—the Holy One of God!"

> But Jesus rebuked him, saying, "Be quiet, and come out of him!"

> And when the unclean spirit had convulsed him and cried out with a loud voice, he came out of him. (Mark 1:23–26 NKJV)

Since the name of Jesus Christ has such power, Satan and his children fear it. They will find all kinds of excuses for not allowing His name to be used in public. They will tell you that the name of Jesus Christ is not to be used in any public forum as doing so violates the church vs. state law. They act as if saying the name of Jesus in public is illegal or taboo.

Sometimes, it appears as if the only politically correct way to use the name of Jesus Christ is when you are expressing the emotion of great anger. Then, it is quite proper to use the name of Jesus Christ!

So when the city, or your neighbor, or whoever prays to the heavenly Father without praying in the name of Jesus, their prayers are no more than just words floating around; they are powerless. The power of our prayers is in the name of our Lord and Savior, Jesus Christ. And unless our prayers have been endorsed in His name, they are powerless.

Jesus told us,

And whatever you ask in My name, that I will do, that the Father may be glorified in the Son. If you ask anything in My name, I will do it. (John 14:13–14 NKJV)

tb *Arrg!* That Tongue!

James 3 tells us a lot about our tongues. Here is a quick overview of this chapter.

Scriptures tells us that our tongues

like to brag—

The tongue is a small part of the body, but it makes great boasts. Boasting can be a symptom of pride and a way of putting others down.

Even so the tongue is a little member and boasts great things. (James 3:5 NKJV)

spread rumors like wildfire—

Consider what happens when a great forest is set on fire by lightning or an unattended campfire. The tongue is also a spark that can start wildfires.

> See how great a forest a little fire kindles! (James 3:5 NKJV)

cause the whole body to rot—

The tongue can create a world of evil among the parts of the body. The tongue can cause corruption of the whole person and can show others this corruption as well.

> And the tongue is a fire, a world of iniquity. The tongue is so set among our members that it defiles the whole body, and sets on fire the course of nature. (James 3:6 NKJV)

affect others—

In fact, it may even be able to corrupt others. Jesus told us the things that come out of the mouth are from the heart.

> But those things which proceed out of the mouth come from the heart, and they defile a man. (Matthew 15:18 NKJV)

cause us to live lives of hellish fire—

Our tongues can set the whole course of our lives on fire with the fire of hell.

> It is set on fire by hell. (James 3:6 NKJV)

cannot be tamed—

James tells us that even though we have the capability to tame beasts, birds, and even reptiles, we cannot tame our tongues.

For every kind of beast and bird, of reptile and creature of the sea, is tamed and has been tamed by mankind. But no man can tame the tongue. (James 3:7–8 NKJV)

are unruly, evil, deadly—

God's Word calls our tongues an unruly evil filled with poison.

It is an unruly evil, full of deadly poison. (James 3:8 NKJV)

are forked like the tongues of serpents—

We praise our Lord and sing worship songs to our heavenly Father, but then we curse our brothers and sisters and gossip with the same tongues. Out of the same mouths come praise of God and cursing of people.

With it we bless our God and Father, and with it we curse men, who have been made in the similitude of God. Out of the same mouth proceed blessing and cursing. My brethren, these things ought not to be so. (James 3:9–10 NKJV)

What a small but powerful member of our physical bodies and our Christian body, the church, our tongues are.

tb True Forgiveness

When someone harms you, you have been instructed by Jesus to forgive that person.

> Take heed to yourselves. If your brother sins against you, rebuke him; and if he repents, forgive him. And if he sins against you seven times in a day, and seven times in a day returns to you saying, "I repent," you shall forgive him. (Luke 17:3–4 NKJV)

This is not a suggestion; it is an instruction, a command if you will. So please forgive those who offend you. Pray for them often. By doing so, you will place them in the hands of God. Forgive them and let God take care of the matter.

True forgiveness is not worrying about what this person does or says about you. It is not having to get back at this person or having to be the first to tell the story to others in hopes you will not look so bad. It is not treating this person in a bad way because that is how he or she treated you. Nor is it ignoring or snubbing him or her because you don't like how you were treated.

No!

True forgiveness is turning the situation over to God and having faith in God's ability to take care of what you have placed in His hands. It is having trust in His willingness to take care of the situation for you. It is having enough faith and trust in God's ability and willingness to take care of you that you allow God to handle the situation the way He sees fit.

Forgiveness is having enough belief in God's desire to do good for you that you take those who offend you off the hot seat, put them in God's care, and leave them there.

You are God's child. Your heavenly Father knows how to take care of all His children, you included. He will guard you, vindicate you, and take care of your revenge for you. He will do so in a way that shows your innocence if you are indeed innocent and will show His great power as well. God's way will bring glory to Himself and will confirm His love for you.

> Beloved do not avenge yourselves, but rather give place to wrath; for it is written, "Vengeance is Mine, I will repay," says the Lord. (Romans 12:19 NKJV)

tb Creations of Art

Ah! Those pieces of art created by such masters as Picasso and Rembrandt. What great pieces of beauty!

They are sought with great fervor by collectors willing to pay large sums for them. They hang the masterpieces in places of honor showing them off to everyone who comes to their homes. Collectors take time to adore the art and will talk about their collections at every opportunity. As they should.

But according to scriptures, God is the Creator of all things, even those great masterpieces. God created the universes, the planets, the stars, and everything in them. He creates sunsets each evening and sunrises each day. He creates the rainbows that come with rain. He created all the flowers, birds, fish, and animals.

But how do we treat the masterpieces God has created? Do we seek them with great fervor? Are we willing to pay any price for them? Have we given God's masterpieces a place of honor in our homes? Do we take time to adore His art? Do we talk about it every time the opportunity arises?

We should.

Is not just one of God's creations much more valuable that all those Picassos and Rembrandts combined?

tb Know God's Will for Your Life

Have you ever wanted to know God's will for your life? Well, here it is. Here is a list that is easy to understand and follow. It was given to those who through Jesus Christ are God's children.

> Rejoice always, pray without ceasing, in everything give thanks; for this is the will of God in Christ Jesus for you. (1 Thessalonians 5:16–18 NKJV)

We are told to be joyful always. Not only on payday Fridays, or only when we open Christmas gifts, or when we get our way. But always.

We are to rejoice in good times and bad times alike. In times of plenty and in times of need. In good health and in bad. Always.

There is always something to be joyful and thankful for even if it is only for having a bed to sleep in or a piece of bread to eat.

We are to pray continually. Not only when we need something, or when we are in trouble, or are sick, but continually—all the time.

"How can this be?" you may ask. "Am I to spend my entire day on my knees in my prayer closet praying to God?

How am I to get anything done? I have a job, a family, chores, responsibilities."

I know—I felt the same way. But then, I remembered that praying to God is really talking with God. So when we pray continually to God, we are actually talking continually with God. Not to God—with God.

We are to talk to God and listen to Him. This is called conversation, the kind of open, honest conversation that enables strong relationships to form and grow. And then, oddly enough, the stronger our relationship grows with God, the more we will talk to Him and will listen for His answers and will converse with Him.

We are to give thanks in all circumstances. All. That means while we are enduring the bad circumstances of life as well as the good ones. Sometimes, the sting of bad circumstances causes us to drop our pretenses and seek God with our entire beings and hearts. Times of despair cause us to bare our souls and be honest with God. They are times we clearly see how God works in our lives.

When we grasp this, being thankful comes naturally.

tb Firstfruits

> Honor the LORD with your possessions,
> and with the firstfruits of all your increase;
> so your barns will be filled with plenty,
> and your vats will overflow with new wine.
> (Proverbs 3:8–10 NKJV)

Yes, I know! There they go again—Christians using scripture to get into your wallet. I hear you.

But wait. This scripture is not to be used that way. It

is a promise from God that if you honor Him with your firstfruits, He will fill your barns to overflowing. If you honor God with the first portions of your income, He will fill your life with blessings far beyond your imagination. Wow!

Sounds simple, doesn't it? It isn't. For some reason, we all have difficulty trusting God with our money. We trust Him with our unsaved family members, for protection from those who harm us, for travel mercies, and for healing. But for some reason, we still find it hard to fully trust God with our money.

How silly of us! God is the owner of everything, even our money. God asks us to give Him back 10 percent of what He has given us and allows us to do as we please with the remaining 90 percent. Mind-blowing or what?

Knowing how hard it is for us to trust Him with our money, God has given us permission to test Him in this area. According to Him, those who are not giving back to Him what He is due are robbing Him, stealing from Him.

But God extends mercy to those who are struggling in this area and asks them to test Him. He wants them to honor Him with their firstfruits so He can in turn bless their socks off! To which again I ask, mind-blowing or what?

> "Will a man rob God? Yet you have robbed Me! But you say, 'In what way have we robbed You?'"

> "In tithes and offerings. You are cursed with a curse for you have robbed Me, even this whole nation."

> "Bring all the tithes into the storehouse, that there may be food in My house, and try Me

now in this," says the LORD of hosts, "If I will not open for you the windows of heaven and pour out for you such blessing, that there will not be room enough to receive it."

"And I will rebuke the devourer for your sakes, so that he will not destroy the fruit of your ground, nor shall the vine fail to bear fruit for you in the field," says the LORD of hosts; "and all nations will call you blessed, for you will be a delightful land," says the LORD of hosts. (Malachi 3:8–12 NKJV)

So, now you can see that those sharing Proverbs 3:9–10 are not asking you for money but rather telling you about a promise from God.

tb When You ...

When you hurt, are weary, tired, and scared, just cling to God, His Word, and His Son and you will find rest. If you know God, you can rest in Him.

Cast your burden on the LORD, and He shall sustain you; He shall never permit the righteous to be moved. (Psalm 55:22 NKJV)

tb The Road of Life

The road of life used to look so steady, clear, and easy to travel. But as I age, I find this has changed. The road of life is now filled with lots of curves, potholes, and stony spots. The road narrows and widens. Some areas of the road are straight allowing for fast-paced, fun-loving styles of living while other areas are slippery and treacherous. Some areas are just downright hard—extremely uphill with little footing.

Yet we are told—no, we are promised—that God will be right there traveling with us on this road of life. And that if we go to Him when we need help, He will be there and help us.

Are you going to God when you need help? When you have to go uphill with very little footing? When you cannot see around that next curve?

No? Why not? Don't know how?

Let me tell you how. First, surrender your life to Jesus. Then, every time you need His guidance, ask Him to help you; He will guide you around that curve or pothole every time you ask.

And he is the only one who can; Jesus is the only way to God and heaven. Many people will tell you otherwise, but they are mistaken. Don't listen to them. Listen to Jesus.

> Jesus said to him, "I am the way, the truth, and the life. No one comes to the Father except through Me." (John 14:6 NKJV)

tb Love Ourselves?

Jesus told us to love others as we love ourselves.

> Jesus said to him, "You shall love the LORD your God with all your heart, with all your

soul, and with all your mind. This is the first and great commandment. And the second is like it: 'You shall love your neighbor as yourself.'" (Matthew 23:37–39 NKJV)

The loving ourselves part of this scripture sets the pattern of how we are to love others. Jesus told us to love others as we love ourselves. So how do you love yourself? Or do you even love yourself?

I know these may seem like strange questions, but unless we love ourselves, we cannot love others. I am not talking about loving ourselves in a selfish way. I am not saying we are to love ourselves in the same fashion we so often see the world love itself. Nor am I suggesting we are to live life on a me-first basis. I'm talking about loving ourselves in a healthy way, a good way, a spiritual way—the same way God and Jesus love us.

Unless you love yourself warts and all, how can you love others with their warts? Until you have love for yourself, you can never really have love for others. You cannot give something you don't have.

Loving yourself is something God wants you to do strange as that may seem.

tb My Sheep

Last night, I was at my sister's house. She and her husband have a few sheep that were grazing in the yard. As we got out of the truck, a mother sheep with her lamb ventured over to check us out. She was not sure who we were, and my speaking to her made her only more unsure. She placed herself between my husband

and me, and her lamb, and looked at us. Not wanting to stress momma and baby, we went into the house and left them alone.

When it was time for us to leave, the sheep were very close to the door. Once again, I tried to approach the herd and found the same response. But when my brother-in-law came out and spoke the words "Come here ladies," the entire herd came running to him. They talked with him and mingled around him. They all wanted to be the closest to him. They had heard their master's voice and wanted to be where he was. They seemed to be smiling as they waited their turns to be handled. Made me think of what Jesus said,

> My sheep hear My voice, and I know them,
> and they follow Me. (John 10:27 NKJV)

These sheep knew the voice of their master and came running when he called. Do you?

tb Satan Is a Liar

> Why is my language not clear to you? Because you are unable to hear what I say. You belong to your father, the devil, and you want to carry out your father's desire. He was a murderer from the beginning, not holding to the truth, for there is no truth in him. When he lies, he speaks his native language, for he is a liar and the father of lies. (John 8:43–44 NIV)

God's Word tells us Satan is a liar. Jesus told us Satan

was the father of lies. The big cheese of all who lie. The liar of all liars. And Jesus told us Satan could not say anything that was not a lie because lying was his native language.

Taking this scripture and letting it settle down deep inside your mind, heart, and soul is very helpful. If you're like me, Satan likes to sit on your shoulder and whisper things like, "You're not good enough to call yourself a Christian" or "Oh really? You really think God can use someone like you?" or "How can Jesus really love someone like you who has done_____?"

And then there is his greatest and sometimes most effective lie—"God doesn't really love you. God doesn't really care about you. Not really! That's why all these bad things keep happening to you."

But if you put John 8:43–44 deep in your heart and soul, you can know without a doubt that what Satan tells you is nothing but lies.

So - if what Satan tells you is nothing but lies, then take what Satan has told you and turn it around.

And you will have the truth.

tb New Projects

It's easy to start a new project. The excitement of something new is so intoxicating that it drives you into action. You can't seem to think of much else. It sits in your craw as my husband would say.

The real test, however, comes in the finishing of the project. In completing what you have started. Most of the time when you're halfway down that new, exciting road, the excitement begins to dull and turn into a humdrumness or maybe even boredom. The newness and intoxication no longer exist.

But we are told to finish the race or project regardless of the level of excitement. In fact, we are told that the way we finish the race or project is just as important as how we started it. God tells us to run the race well and to finish strong.

God will guide us all, as we race down that path called life. And He will tell us how to finish strong. But we need to look for His guidance. We need to read His Word. And we need to keep our eyes on our great Shepherd. For it is only when we do these things, that we can and will, run our race well and finish strong.

Thank you, Lord, for helping us do what You have asked us to do.

> Therefore, since we are surrounded by such a great cloud of witnesses, let us lay aside every weight, and the sin which so easily ensnares us, and let us run with endurance the race that is set before us, looking unto Jesus, the author and finisher of our faith, who for the joy that was set before Him endured the cross, despising the shame, and has sat down at the right hand of the throne of God. (Hebrews 12:1–2 NKJV)

tb But Lord?

Now there was a certain disciple at Damascus named Ananias; and to him the Lord said in a vision, "Ananias." And he said, "Here I am, Lord."

So the Lord said to him, "Arise and go to the street called Straight, and inquire at the house of Judas for one called Saul of Tarsus, for behold, he is praying. And in a vision he has seen a man named Ananias coming in and putting his hand on him, so that he might receive his sight."

Then Ananias answered, "Lord, I have heard from many about this man, how much harm he has done to Your saints in Jerusalem. And here he has authority from the chief priests to bind all who call on Your name."

But the Lord said to him, "Go for he is a chosen vessel of Mine to bear My name before Gentiles, kings, and the children of Israel. For I will show him how many things he must suffer for My name's sake." (Acts 9:10–16 NKJV)

When I read this passage, I often wonder how I'd react if God requested the same from me. Would I blindly obey God knowing He has my best interests in mind? Knowing He will protect me as I obey His request?

Or would I react in the same manner as Ananias did?

How would I react if God told me to mentor someone I felt was a great threat to myself and fellow Christians?

I cannot say I would not question God as Ananias

did. Nor can I say I wouldn't try to run away from God's assignment as Jonah did. As if we can hide from God.

But I have recently had a small taste of such a request, and I'm pleased to say I was obedient to God's request. While I was being obedient to my Lord, I heard the sorrowful cries of someone whose past would not let him go. Of someone who was truly remorseful of how he had once lived. Of how he had once treated God's people. They were the cries of someone who, like Paul, was once a Saul of Tarsus.

Since that experience, I read this scripture from a different point of view, a new twist. I see Ananias's viewpoint and maybe even Paul's, the man who was once Saul, a hunter of Jesus's followers.

What better way to display Jesus's love for others than to love them even if they were once like the man named Saul.

tb So Who's Your Daddy?

> Do not call anyone on earth your father;
> for One is your Father, He who is in heaven.
> (Matthew 23:9 NKJV)

Jesus gave us these words. And to those whose father is not the heavenly Father, Jesus had these words.

> Jesus said to them, "If God were your Father,
> you would love Me, for I proceeded forth
> and came from God; nor have I come of
> Myself, but He sent Me."

"Why do you not understand My speech? Because you are not able to listen to My word. You are of your father the devil, and the desires of your father you want to do. He was a murderer from the beginning, and does not stand in the truth, because there is no truth in him. When he speaks a lie, he speaks from his own resources, for he is a liar and the father of it." (John 8:42–44 NKJV)

So who is your father? Is He the Father of truth or the father of lies?

Is He the heavenly Father or the murderer?

Is your inheritance found in your Father's mansion or in the pits of hell?

This is the only time you are able to choose who your father is. The ball's in your court.

tb Dark Nights

While traveling along a stretch of I-75 on a dark, cloudy night, I noticed how brilliant the headlights of our truck were and how well the markers along the road were reflecting that light. I realized that it was the darkness which caused the markers to reflect light so well.

And so it is with our spiritual walk with Jesus. Only when the night is the darkest does Jesus's light shine the brightest. The darker the night, the greater His light. The darkness causes His light to bounce off God's reflectors. It is only on these dark, cloudy nights, when we cannot clearly see our way that we must look for God's reflectors to help us find our way.

Thank You, Lord, for those dark, cloudy nights and for Your reflectors—Your guidance.

It Can *Not* Be Earned

Acceptance and forgiveness cannot be earned; they must be given.

Approval and acceptance are not the same. We can earn approval from others by what we say and do. We all know how to do this and have done so. Students who do well on tests earn the approval of their teachers. Athletes who excel earn the approval of their teammates and coaches.

However, acceptance is given to you. It is a gift. You can do and say, and do and say, but unless those for whom you are doing all this doing and saying accept you, all of it is in vain. You cannot earn their acceptance; they must give it to you.

And so it is with forgiveness. You can ask and even beg for someone's forgiveness until you are blue in the face. Or until the cows come home. Or until your teeth fall out from old age. You can try to earn others' forgiveness by standing on your head or being their personal slave. But unless they are willing to give you their forgiveness, you cannot have it. Just like acceptance, forgiveness is a gift to be freely given; it cannot be bought or earned.

Our forgiveness from God is a gift He freely gives us through our sacrificial Lamb, Jesus Christ. The moment we accept God's gift of salvation, we are given another gift—His acceptance.

God accepts us just as we are, sin-filled and all. Through

the blood of Jesus, He picks us up, wipes our faces, and accepts us into His family as one of His children. He opens our eyes and ears so we can see Him in His glory and hear of His love for us through His Word. This too is His gift to those willing to accept it.

> Every good and every perfect gift is from above, and comes down from the Father of lights, with whom there is no variation or shadow of turning. (James 1:17 NKJV)

tb Surprised?

Why are we so surprised that Satan is after our country? And why are we, the church, so laid back about Satan's siege of what used to be known as one nation under God? Have we not learned from the reign of people such as Nero, Hitler, and other evil men, that Satan will use such humans to take over nations? Especially those that claim to belong to God? Nations who proclaim that Jesus is the Messiah? *Their* Messiah?

Have we so quickly forgotten how Satan wants to rid the earth of God's people? Or are we so naive as to believe this type of behavior, this type of cruel dictatorship, will never happen again?

Our country was founded as a Christian nation for and by people who desired a country that worshipped and revered God. A country based on Christian values. A people who desired a land where they could openly worship God and His Son, Jesus. A land where they could openly teach their young the scriptures and the ways of godly living.

I have read that in the early hours of our country, the

Bible was used in public schools as a reading primer. Yes—the Bible was used to teach students how to read. History lessons taught in public schools were taken from the Old Testament. History shows us that this was a time when morals were taught and lived. People respected others as well as themselves, lived by the golden rule (Luke 6:31), and revered life.

America, a country founded by godly men so God would be worshipped, has moved far from Him.

Have we not learned? If not from our Bibles then from history? God will remove His hand from us as a nation if we, His people, turn from His face. Not maybe. Not if. But will.

Do we not believe God when He tells us that if we continue to knowingly live in sin, He will give us over to our depraved minds?

> And even as they did not like to retain God in their knowledge, God gave them over to a debased mind, to do those things which are not fitting; being filled with all unrighteousness, sexual immorality, wickedness, covetousness, maliciousness; full of envy, murder, strife, deceit, evil-mindedness; they are whisperers, backbiters, haters of God, violent, proud, boasters, inventors of evil things, disobedient to parents, undiscerning, untrustworthy, unloving, unforgiving, unmerciful; who, knowing the righteous judgment of God, that those who practice such things are deserving of death, not only do the same but also approve of those who practice them. (Romans 1:28–32 NKJV)

Does this not sound like the America of today? And

yet what have we done? Are we as a nation living a life of righteousness? Do we as a nation have a lifestyle that is pleasing to God? That is worthy of Jesus Christ's blood? Do we not believe God's Word when He tells us that if we continue to live in sin once we know better, we no longer live under the covering of our sin sacrifice?

For if we sin willfully after we have received the knowledge of the truth, there no longer remains a sacrifice for sins, but a certain fearful expectation of judgment, and fiery indignation which will devour the adversaries. (Hebrews 10:26–27 NKJV)

Or could it be that we no longer care?

tb So Much Religion!

Baptist. Methodist. Presbyterian. Church of God. Nazarene Church. Church of Christ. Catholic Church. Nondenominational Church. Calvinist.

Premillennial Postmillennial.

Rapture. No rapture.

Hymns. Praise songs. Live music. Recorded music. No music.

Worship on Sundays. Worship on Saturdays.

New King James Version. Old King James Version. NIV. NCV. ESB.

Bibles on electronic devices. Bibles on paper.

Sit to read scriptures. Stand to read scriptures.

Talk and visit in the sanctuary. No talking in the sanctuary.

Okay to make notes in your Bible, your owner's manual. Not okay to write in the Bible, the Word of God.

Tongues are real. Tongues are fake.

Anoint with oil. Anointing with oil is no longer necessary because of Jesus's blood. Spiritual gifts are very much alive. Spiritual gifts were for the saints of the past.

Work hard for your provisions. Rely solely on God to provide.

To be healed. Not to be healed.

You are holy and filled with God's righteousness. You are only a sinner saved by grace whose works are a filthy rag.

Just ask God for anything you want and He will give it to you. God is not a vending machine.

God has predestined those He will save. Salvation is for all who will receive it.

You must go and do. No, sit and wait.

Believe this. Don't believe that.

That is legalism. That is too liberal.

Keep yourself pure and live a righteous life. You are not to be a hermit; live in a manner that is accepting to the world.

So much religion! What is a Christian to do?

Ask God.

tb Easily Led Astray

Recently, I watched a clip from the *Left Behind* series. A reporter had been chosen by Nicolae, who was the Antichrist, to do some public relations work for him. Prior to the UN meeting, the reporter was contacted by some who were known as the Haters. This group of Christians shared the gospel with him. Later that day, he prayed to God and accepted Jesus Christ as his Savior.

Fast forward to the UN meeting. Nicolae and the reporter are at the meeting. In the beginning, all is relatively well. Then Nicolae stands and takes charge of the meeting. He tells about the plans he has for the world and the changes he wants to make.

One man stands and opposes Nicolae's plans. He feels Nicolae is trying to become a dictator. Without any emotion, Nicolae takes a pistol from one of the guards and kills the man. As an example of what happens to those who oppose him, Nicolae kills the man seated next to the man who opposed his plan, as well as the guard standing nearby.

As all sit in shock, Nicolae very calmly tells them that what they really saw was the man who had opposed him shoot both the man seated next to him and the guard. He tells them that this had happened before he had time to defend any of the victims.

As all were leaving the meeting, the reporter turns to a woman and exclaims, "Wow! I can't believe what just happened in there!"

The woman replies, "I know. Isn't it terrible! Why did that man shoot everyone?"

The reporter and the woman had witnessed the same event, but she believed things had happened the way Nicolae said they had happened. The woman believed Nicolae's lies. The woman believed what the Antichrist had told her to believe because her spiritual eyes were closed.

Yet the reporter knew the truth. When he had received Jesus Christ as his Savior, his spiritual eyes had been opened and he saw what really happened, not what the Antichrist said had happened.

Replace the woman with the unsaved in this world and you will see why this world—why America—is so easily led astray. Their spiritual eyes are still closed.

The coming of the lawless one is according to the working of Satan, with all power, signs, and lying wonders, and with all unrighteous deception among those who perish, because they did not receive the love of the truth, that they might be saved. (2 Thessalonians 2:9–10 NKJV)

tb My Own Chores

Recently, I have been struggling with a very busy life. It seems there are many things others are asking me to do. Fitting these things into my already full schedule is squeezing out a few things I would like to do. So to my shame, as I moved hurriedly from task to task, I found myself saying, "I have my own chores. Can't you people see I'm maxed out? Why must I do all the work? Must I take care of everyone else's stuff?"

One day, my pastor reminded me that we were to be living sacrifices. *Living sacrifices.* Those words echoed in my mind as I trudged through my chores. Not dead sacrifices. Living sacrifices.

Then just as if someone had turned on a light, I understood what *living sacrifices* meant. The tasks I was half-heartedly trudging through were not really for the people who had asked me to do them. No. They were for Jesus!

The scripture that says whatever you find to do with your hands, do it as if unto the Lord filled my thoughts. Wow! These people were not asking me to do these things—Jesus was.

As a new week unfolds, the chores and the busyness are still there, but my thoughts are different. I am now saying, "Thank You, Jesus, for believing I'm capable of handling the many chores You have given me to do."

As I move from task to task completing all Jesus's requests, I now ask, "Please Lord, help me do these chores well. Help me do them to Your standards. I will give You the glory for them."

What a difference!

tb No Need

There is no need for us to sneak a bite of the fruit on the Tree of Knowledge of Good and Evil.

No. God will freely give us this knowledge of Him through Jesus Christ.

All we have to do is open our Bibles!

tb Nonsense

Among Satan's most effective lies are that you are too dirty for Jesus, that you must clean yourself up before you can go to Him, that you must start doing right before God will even think about loving you.

Nonsense.

Jesus loves you just the way you are, dirt and all.

tb A Letter of Resignation

To: Satan

Cc: Satan's Demons, Satan's Children

Please consider this as my letter of resignation effective immediately. I have accepted a position with Jesus Christ and will be working for Him full time.

This change in employment will enable me to honor my Lord with all I am, all I have, and all I will be.

Should you have any questions, please see John 3:16–17.

Signed:

A new creation in Christ!

tb Our Filter

Jesus is not only our Savior; He is our filter as well. Because of the blood He shed on the cross, He is our sacrificial sin Lamb. As such, He filters sin from our lives, which allows God to look on us as righteous, not unrighteous. God views us as righteous only while we are under the blood of Jesus. Without the blood of Jesus, no one is righteous.

> As it is written: "There is none righteous, no not one." (Romans 3:10 NKJV)

This filtering away of sin allows us to stand before God's throne. The thought of being before the throne of an almighty and powerful yet loving God is quite humbling. But since Jesus's blood filters away my sin, I can go before God's throne as one who is righteous. Wow!

And Jesus does this for me.

He willingly went to the cross as my sacrificial sin Lamb and shed His blood for me. Without the shedding of blood, there could be no remission of sin. Without the shedding of blood, there could be no purification. And no one could be saved because none is righteous without the blood of Jesus making him or her so.

> And according to the law almost all things are purified with blood, and without shedding of blood there is no remission. (Hebrews 9:22 NKJV)

(Please read all of Hebrews 9.)

The blood of Jesus is not only our filter through which God can look down upon us, but it is also the only way to heaven. The only way to God's throne. <u>The only way.</u>

> Jesus said to him, "I am the way, the truth, and the life. No one comes to the Father except through Me." (John 14:6 NKJV)

tb I Had No Idea!

Dear Jesus,

When we first met, I had no idea how much You would mean to me. I could not imagine how great Your love for me was. You willingly laid down Your life so I could find mine.

You have given me stories to help me with life. You have made promises to me and have kept them. You are always with me. You have never thrown me under the bus or walked away from me.

You always listen when I talk with You, and You are always willing to answer my questions. You pick me up, dust off my knees, kiss my forehead, and give me a word of encouragement every time I fall.

And, as if that were not enough, You make sure God knows that I belong to You, that You and I have a relationship, that I am a soul washed in Your blood.

Thank you, Jesus, for all You have done for me. I love You with a love I have never known before. I had no idea when we first met, just how much I would grow to love you.

tb Look What I Found!

But I know whom I have believed and am persuaded that He is able to keep what I've committed to Him against that day.

I Know Whom I Have Believed (Hymnal page 344).

> For this reason I also suffer these things; nevertheless I am not ashamed, for I know whom I have believe and am persuaded that He is able to keep what I have committed to Him until that Day. (2 Timothy 1:12 NKJV)

How cool is that?

tb Better with Age

Things become better with age.

Some people say this about fine wines. Others about cheese. Still others about antiques. But having a heart for music, I say that a well-made instrument definitely falls into that category.

In my favorite music store, I was able to play my violin with a fifty-year-old bow. Its horsehairs had been yellowed by many years of rosin. But oh my, how wonderfully the bow fit my hand, and what balance! I sensed the richness of its greatness as it flowed over the strings. What a treasure.

The violin bows of today are just not made like those of yesteryear. Yes, it was a magnificent, old bow that had had lots of use, but it still had purpose, worth. It may not be used as much as it once was; it may find itself sitting on the shelf a little more than it used to. But it still produces a sound so sweet that you can almost smell it. The music it produces fills the room with an old-world richness that soothes the ear.

Just like the violin bow, we too are aging. We are all sitting on that aging bus. Some of us are sitting in the front while others are in the rear, but we are all sitting in that same bus of aging. This I can guarantee.

And as we age, we are sometimes replaced with those who are younger. Those who have not had as much use. That happens at work, in our family life, and yes, even in our church. *Ouch!*

But though we may feel like we are finding ourselves on the shelf more and more as we age, though we may feel we are no longer useful, we are still very valuable and useful to God. As we age, we gain a lot of insight into life and have learned a lot about God. The wisdom of our aging years is a great gift from God. And we are to share this wisdom, our gift from God, with those who are younger. When we do, we are doing what the Lord has asked us to do.

You may view your aging in a negative way, but God views your aging as a form of righteousness; He calls your gray hair a crown of splendor (the NKJV says glory).

> Gray hair is a crown or splendor; it is attained
> by a righteous life. (Proverbs 16:31 NIV)

God views you as still having purpose and worth. He feels that as long as you have air in your lungs, you are still valuable, useful, and able to work for His kingdom.

And who are we to doubt God's judgment?

tb The Silhouette

I had just finished feeding the last horse and had turned toward the gate. The sun was lowering in the western sky casting ribbons of sunlight over the paddock. I could just about make out the silhouette of my dog, Levi, sitting at the gate patiently waiting for me to return.

He did not run off, or chase the cat, or do any of those other things dogs do. He was just sitting there patiently. Waiting. Ever so patiently. Waiting.

Even to this day, I can still see his silhouette in the western sky of a late summer's day sitting there by the gate watching and waiting for my return.

And as I recall how patiently he sat by the gate just waiting and watching, I wonder, *Is this what Jesus sees when He looks at me? One of His own watching and waiting for His return? Patiently and attentively waiting?*

tb Subtle but Powerful

Ah those old sitcoms. I have been watching some of those old ones—*Gilligan's Island. Mr. Ed. Gomer Pyle.*

Bewitched was on as I sat for my nightly icing. Daryl had just come home from a hard day's work at the office. The house which was clean, neat, and tidy was also very much the style typical for that era. Samantha was busy in the kitchen cooking dinner for her husband. The scene was a typical home life for a married couple.

As Daryl was telling Samantha of his day at the office, he walked to a small breakfast bar just off the kitchen. While he talked with his wife, he did something I had never noticed before—he poured himself an alcoholic drink.

Now, I'm not harping about drinking alcohol, but on the fact that this sitcom was supposed to be a family show. One of the main characters nonchalantly pours himself a drink as if this were a normal after-work activity for families.

How subtle is this nonverbal suggestion. And yet how powerful. And how like Satan! Putting in small gestures. Small undertones. Subtle and yet powerful. Oh what a crafty one Satan is! And oh how persistent!

tb Nutrients

Our spiritual lives are like flowers. The moment we receive Jesus Christ as our personal Savior, we become seeds planted in fertile soil. God sends His Son to shine

His light on us and His Word to rain on us. Then we are fertilized with the Holy Spirit.

Those who willingly accept and embrace these nutrients will grow into large, strong plants. Shoots of new growth can be seen, and from these shoots, flowers will spring forth. (You will know them by their fruits.)

As we continue to take in our nutrients—God's Son, His Word, and the Holy Spirit—our flowers will open, become fuller, and end up in full bloom. When we allow God's nutrients to mature us into fully blooming flowers, God can and will use us. Our full blooms will attract others; they will come over to admire our beauty. Some may even find our beauty is so great that they will want to clip us and take us home. They will want to enjoy our beauty for more than a day.

While in full bloom, we can bring joy and peace to those who are mourning, hurting, and in need of joy and peace. We can be that one beautiful thing in the life of someone whose life is filled with bleakness and despair.

But as we are promised, our blooming flowers will not be in full bloom forever. God's Word tells us that there is a time and a season for all things.

> To everything there is a season, a time for every purpose under heaven. (Ecclesiastes 3:1 NKJV)

So while there is a time for you to bloom, there will also be a time for your blooms to fall off. A time for you to stand as a plant without its flowers. But don't despair. God has a reason for this. The time that you are a plant without flowers is a season when you don't have to sustain full, rich, blooming flowers. It is a season of rest and renewal. A time when you are to just take in God's nutrients and grow. A time to prepare to bloom again.

And the next time you do, your blooms will be even larger, stronger, and more brilliant.

tb John 2

Have you read John 2:1–11 lately? Those of us who know our Bibles will say this passage is about Jesus's first miracle—turning water into wine at a wedding. And they are right. Jesus turned ordinary water into fantastic wine.

But I see more in this scripture. Could this passage reflect salvation? Could it be an analogy of someone whose soul was once lost but is now saved?

Lost souls could be considered as common and plentiful as water. That is until they are touched by the Master's hand. Until they are touched by Jesus. Then, water is turned into something like a fine wine that is so special, the host asked the bridegroom if he had saved the best wine for the end of the reception instead of serving it at the beginning.

> When the master of the feast had tasted the water that was made wine, and did not know where it came from (but the servants who had drawn the water knew) the master of the feast called the bridegroom. And he said to him, "Every man at the beginning sets out the good wine, and when the guests have well drunk, then the inferior. You have kept the good wine until now!" (John 2:9–10 NKJV)

When Jesus touches your life, when He has become your Savior, He changes you from something ordinary into something special.

He changes you from a sinner bound for hell into one of God's children bound for heaven.

That's a great miracle!

tb Memorial Day

In Exodus 12:1–13, God told His people to put the blood of the lamb on the doorposts of their homes so as He traveled Egypt slaying the firstborn of everything—man and beast—He would see the lamb's blood and pass over those homes without touching the firstborn of anything there.

When God saw the lamb's blood on a doorpost, He knew the people inside belonged to Him. God saw the blood as a sign that this household was filled with His people. That protected them from death.

> Now the blood shall be a sign for you on the houses where you are. And when I see the blood, I will pass over you; and the plague shall not be on you to destroy you when I strike the land of Egypt. (Exodus 12:13 NKJV)

Then God told them to make that day a memorial day.

> So this day shall be to you a memorial; and you shall keep it as a feast to the LORD throughout your generations. You shall

keep it as a feast by an everlasting ordinance.
(Exodus 12:14 NKJV)

Note: The NIV calls it a time of celebration, a lasting ordinance.

Today, God is telling His people to put the Lamb's blood on the doorposts of their hearts so when the destroyer sees the blood, he will know that Jesus Christ, the Son of God, is the Lord of their lives and that Jesus Christ sits on the thrones of their hearts. The Lamb's blood on the doorposts of their hearts is public proof that those hearts have been cleansed by the Lamb's blood and are protected from the destroyer.

When you have painted the doorposts of your heart with the blood of your sacrificial Lamb, Jesus Christ, you have sealed your heart as one that belongs to God.

> Now He who establishes us with you in Christ and has anointed us is God, who also has sealed us and given us the Spirit in our hearts as a guarantee. (2 Corinthians 1:21–22 NKJV)

tb Truth for Today

Today, people are so hungry for the truth. They are looking to and fro, here and there and everywhere for directions and help. They Bing and Google and Yahoo their way through life searching for the answers to their questions.

TV is congested with people telling you how to handle your money, how to look younger, how to enjoy being older, to live healthier, be more buff, and how to cook the latest cuisine craze. Radiating with an aura of expertise, the hosts of such shows appear to know what they are talking about, and people pay hundreds to hear what they are saying.

How sad. The only thing those who are looking for the real truth need to do is accept Jesus Christ as their personal Savior. And then open their Bibles and read them.

God will supply them with all the information, wisdom, and guidance they could ever need. All it will cost them is the price of a good Bible and the time to read it. God will supply the rest.

People are so hungry for the truth. And God has promised us He will freely give us the truth. All we have to do is ask.

If any of you lacks wisdom, let him ask of God, who gives to all liberally and without reproach, and it will be given to him. (James 1:5 NKJV)

tb Young Azaleas

We had been without rain for about two weeks. I had to water my young azaleas, which as all gardeners know require a lot of water.

I set my hose on shower and watered my thirsty, droopy azaleas. I made sure each received a generous amount of water. Those poor, thirsty plants.

While I was watering them, I saw the plants lifting their leaves as if they were using them to help drink all the water they could. As the little limbs began to lift skyward, the entire plant seemed to say, "Thank you."

This is how worship is supposed to be. It was as if the plants were worshipping God and thanking Him for the life-saving water.

Hmmm. Their life-saving water. Water that gives life. Like Living Water? Sound like someone you know?

While standing there with hose in hand, I wondered what color each plant would be. I had planted them in good soil. Given them continual feedings of fertilizer. Placed them in an area with adequate sun and shade. Kept them watered. Because of this care, I should see my azaleas in full bloom next spring. Yea!

This is how it is for those who know Jesus as their Savior, for those who are Christians. God plants them in fertile soil, His Word. He fertilizes them with the Holy Spirit. He gives them the light of His Son, Jesus Christ, whose blood waters them with the Living Water. Then they bloom with the fruits of the Spirit.

Can't you imagine what this must look like from God's viewpoint in heaven? Can't you see God smiling with great pleasure as He takes in the beauty of all His people blooming in many colors? Can't you just hear Him saying, "Yea!"?

tb No Hidden Love

> Better is open rebuke than hidden love. (Proverbs 27:5 NIV)

> See to it brothers, that none of you has a sinful, unbelieving heart that turns away from the living God. But encourage one another daily, as long as it is called Today, so that none of you may be hardened by sin's deceitfulness. (Hebrews 3:12–13 NIV)

God's Word tells us that at times, we are to lovingly exhort our Christian brothers and sisters, speaking with them in love about their choices should their actions or lifestyles reflect a turning away from God. And *lovingly* is the key word here.

Yes, I know. At first, this sounds harsh, but they may not know or understand just how harmful their actions are to you, to others, and even to themselves. They may not see how their actions or unrighteous lifestyles are hindering their Christian walks. How their actions may be destroying others' ability to see Jesus Christ in them.

If you along with some of your Christian brothers and sisters were standing on the bank of an alligator-filled river, and you saw they were about to jump in, would you say nothing? Would you just run away not wanting to see anyone eaten by alligators?

Or would you warn them of the unseen danger? Would you warn them that their actions might be fatal?

I think you would care enough about them to warn them of the danger that you can clearly see, but they cannot. And so it should be with our spiritual lives.

This is not a license to kill; we are not to bowl over our Christian brothers and sisters. Nor is this is not a license to gossip. We find strict instructions on the proper way to carry out this warning in Matthew 18:15–17.

Scripture gives us the proper way to exhort those we love. If we follow this formula, we will gain the love of our Christian brothers and sisters, as well as their trust. They will know we care for them and are looking out for their welfare.

Jesus tells us,

If your brother sins against you, go and show
him his fault, just between the two of you. If
he listens to you, you have won your brother
over. (Matthew 18:15 NIV)

A word of caution here though. Don't allow yourself
to become haughty, or think that you are better, holier,
or more religious than they are. For such things smell of
pride and;

Scripture says pride comes before a fall.

Pride goes before destruction, a haughty
spirit before a fall. (Proverbs 16:18 NIV)

We all have sinned. All!

This righteousness from God comes through
faith in Jesus Christ to all who believe. There
is no difference, for all have sinned and fall
short of the glory of God, and are justified
freely by his grace through the redemption
that came by Christ Jesus. (Romans 3:22–
24 NIV)

And, you cannot recognize the danger that lies in front
of those you are warning, unless you have struggled with
the same thing at some time be it now or in the past.

Please remember that.

tb Full-Care Doggy Kennel

Just call me the Shady Hills full-care doggy kennel. Yeppers! I have a doggy kennel going on.

Two members of my Christian family are out of town and have asked me to care for their dogs. I love dogs. They are the best. So when someone needs a free dog sitter, I'm in.

So, 2 visiting dogs + 2 resident dogs = 1 instant doggy kennel.

And in my instant doggy kennel, I have dogs of different breeds, colors, sizes, hair length, and temperament. Some are more laid back than others. The smallest is the most assertive. Go figure.

Since each dog has individual needs, I make sure each dog is cared for in a way that meets his needs. One dog eats only canned food. The other dog needs daily brushing. My personal dog is aged and needs help up the steps. While a visiting dog needs to be walked on a leash. And yet another, needs to run and run.

Sometimes, these dogs will do naughty things. Like chasing the cat. Or stalking the chickens. Or digging holes in the yard. And then, sometimes they will do the worst thing ever—dumpster diving in the kitchen garbage. That's a really big no-no in our household. Danger lurks in the kitchen garbage. The dogs are reprimanded for such naughty behavior, with the exception of chasing cats. For unlike city cats, country cats will turn around face the dogs and swat them on their snouts.

I love the dogs at all times. When they are on their best behavior and when they aren't. When they are naughty and when they are nice. When they have special needs and when they don't. I love them all.

And I love them all the time with no reserve. Each one is different, but my love for each is the same. I have unconditional love for them.

Hmmm. Wait. Doesn't that sound familiar? Like maybe it's the way God loves us all?

We all are individuals with our own needs, some more than others. Some of our needs are special. Some are to be given in different ways and others in normal ways. Some of us are always on our good behavior while others of us are always dumpster diving.

But God loves you as much as He loves me. His love is the same for us all. No favorites.

Yes, there are times when we misbehave. Times when we chase the chickens or dig holes in the yard. But that doesn't stop God from loving us.

God loves us unconditionally. He loves us whether our needs are many or few. He loves us when He has to walk us on a leash or when He can turn us loose to run. When we do as He asks, or when we ignore His requests.

God still loves us. Always. Unconditionally. And He means that.

And - all God asks from us in return is the same thing I ask from my dogs—to love Him back.

tb Mr. Gopher Turtle

What's the cat playing with? Is it a gopher turtle? Let's go see. Yes it is! Oh, what fun the cat is having by taunting him. And now the dog is showing some interest. So for his own safety, I need to take Mr. Gopher Turtle back to the woods.

However, my approach coupled with the closeness of the cat and the dog must have made Mr. Gopher Turtle feel surrounded and threatened. Because he started hissing at us.

When we did not react to the hissing, Mr. Gopher Turtle did something I never knew gopher turtles could do—he started bouncing up and down in place. He was bouncing so hard that he began bouncing around in a circle. He hissed at us as hard as he could. And bounced at us as hard as he could bounce. This strange behavior did catch us off guard. The dog, the cat, and I stood there watching this turtle acting weird.

After a few minutes of this behavior of oddly bouncing and hissing, Mr. Gopher Turtle stopped and looked back at us. Seeing that we were not making any moves to retreat, the frightened turtle just sucked himself right into his shell. *Sureeeettt!* Just like that, Mr. Gopher Turtle was gone.

Doesn't that sound like someone else we know? Maybe Satan? He will hiss at us and bounce at us up and down so hard that he bounces in circles to intimidate and frighten us.

But if we stand fast covered with the blood of our Savior, Jesus, we will not be so easily intimidated or frightened. We will be able to just stand there watching Satan acting weird.

And when he sees we're not paying attention to his bouncing and hissing, just as Mr. Gopher Turtle did, Satan will suck himself back up in his shell. *Sureeettt!* Just like that, he will be gone.

tb Afraid of What God Wants You to Do?

Are you afraid to do what God has asked you to do? Are you afraid He might ask you to do something you can't do? Or maybe something you will not like doing?

Are you concerned that God will ask you to move from place to place when in fact you're a homebody? Maybe you're concerned He will ask you to serve Him in the backwoods when you detest long commutes and smelly campfires?

If that's the case, look at what Satan asked you to do in your former life. In your life before you accepted Jesus as your personal Savior. Remember how Satan asked you to do all the things you now find distasteful? Remember how he asked you to travel to places you wouldn't go to today? Remember how you did all those things willingly?

When you compare the things God may ask you to do with the things you did for Satan, how bad could God's requests be? God will ask you to do things that will bring glory to Him and strengthen your walk with Him. He will equip you to do what He asks you to do. He will protect you and make a way for you to do them because He loves you and wants you to succeed.

On the other hand, Satan asks you to do things that only feed his pride. Satan does not equip you for his work. He couldn't care less if you failed. If you died and went to hell while you were serving him, you'd be nothing more to him than just another casualty.

Please always remember that God will never ask you to do things *without* the help of Jesus. While, Satan will never ask you to do things *with* the help of Jesus.

tb Are You Unbroken?

While singing out of the hymnal one day, I was having a hard time holding it open. Thy hymnal appeared to have a mind of its own; it kept changing pages and even attempted to close. That made it very difficult for me to sing.

On the podium was the hymnal our praise team leader was singing from. It was just sitting there, wide open, the needed pages fully exposed and easy to read.

Hmmm. Why the difference?

The hymnal I was using had not been used very much. It was fairly new, and the binding was stiff. The pages would flip to wherever they wanted to almost as if the hymnal had a mind of its own and was being rebellious. Singing from this stiff, unyielding hymnal was hard.

But the hymnal on the podium had been used a lot, and its binding was much more flexible, maybe even a little broken in some places. Because of this, its pages were yielding and easy to use. And because it was easy to use, it was being used more often. It stayed open to the place you needed while my hymnal was rebellious and did not. It was as if my hymnal didn't want to be used and the leader's hymnal did.

Just like that praise team leader's hymnal, you must be just a little broken before you can be used. You must be broken in spirit so you can be useful for God's work and for His children. If your binding, your will, is not broken, if you are stiff willed, you will be just like my hymnal—unyielding and rebellious. You'll be living your way, not God's way, and making it difficult for Him to use you.

But if you are of a broken spirit, God will be able to use you with ease. You will lie wide open waiting for God to turn you to the page He wants you to be on. You will be inviting Him to use you. Because of your brokenness, God will be able to change the pages in your life without a lot of trouble. He will be able to turn you to a page, and you will obediently lie there waiting until He turns the page.

Because your brokenness will allow you to live like an open book, people will be drawn to you and will see Jesus's holiness. They will want to be with you and listen to what you say about God and Jesus.

Which hymnal are you? The one with the binder that is broken in some areas? Or the stiff one with a mind of its own?

tb In All Things

Rejoice always, pray without ceasing, in everything give thanks; for this is the will of God in Christ Jesus for you. (1 Thessalonians 5:16–18 NKJV)

We are to rejoice always, pray without ceasing, and give thanks in all circumstances including

- financial hardships
- broken bones
- illnesses
- difficult family relationships
- the passing of loved ones
- heartaches
- rocky marriages
- struggles with addictions
- failed businesses
- wrongly treated by others
- in fear

That is, in all circumstances.

Thanking God for such hard circumstances seems to be an oxymoron, doesn't it? But listen to this.

When we are enduring hardships, we can best see

God's handiwork. Without such circumstances, we are usually too busy living the mountaintop experiences to see what God can do in our lives.

But when we are under the terrific force of hardships, we tend to watch for God's lead with a little more diligence, and we thus see more of His blessings, leading, and mercy.

They are times when we can see God's love for us with much clearer vision.

When I see how much He loves me, I cannot help but be thankful.

How about you?

tb Sin Causes Separation and Fear

> And they heard the sound of the LORD God walking in the garden in the cool of the day, and Adam and his wife hid themselves from the presence of the LORD God among the trees of the garden.
>
> Then the LORD God called to Adam and said to him, "Where are you?"
>
> So he said, "I heard Your voice in the garden, and I was afraid because I was naked; and I hid myself." (Genesis 3:8–10 NKJV)

Until that time, Adam and Eve had enjoyed a very close relationship with God. They had lived lives of innocence and trust. But once they had eaten the forbidden fruit, they lost that extreme closeness with God and became fearful. When God came looking for them, they tried to hide from

Him. Their sinful act had caused their separation from God, which caused fear.

We do the same when we sin—we lose that extreme closeness with God and become fearful. We try to hide from Him because we are no longer innocent. But what does God do? Just as He did with Adam and Eve, He comes to us and asks, "Where are you?" And just as He did with Adam and Eve, He continues to provide for us.

But the amazing part of this story is that God wants us back in His garden even after we have eaten the forbidden fruit. I hear Him softly saying, "My child, I want you to live with Me for eternity. So here is My Sacrificial Lamb for your sins. His name is Jesus Christ. He is My Only Son, in whom I am well pleased. Please accept Him as your Savior so you can once again have a close, intimate relationship with Me always. That is what I long for because I love you."

tb We Reap What We Sow

Do not be deceived. God is not mocked; for whatever a man sows, that he will also reap. (Galatians 6:7 NKJV)

Is it too hard to believe this scripture? Give it a test.

Go up to people and act kindly to them. Smile at them and tell them something good and positive. What do they do? Do they respond with kindness?

Then go up to people and act angry at them. Speak negative words to them. Use a gruff tone when speaking with them. Watch their reactions. Watch their body language. What did you see? Anger?

Then tell people you love them. Give them hugs and kisses or even just compliments. What was their reaction? Did they hug you back? Or break out in big smiles?

Seems like our Bible is right, doesn't it? That we reap what we sow? Applying this scripture to life, we would see someone who

- sows love and reaps love,
- sows help and reaps help,
- sows anger and reaps anger,
- sows selfishness and reaps selfishness,
- sows tenderness and reaps tenderness,
- sows honesty and reaps honesty,
- sows trust and reaps trust,
- sows pride and reaps pride, and so on.

You can usually tell what you are sowing by what you are reaping. Have you found people to be cordial? Friendly? Smiling?

Or have you been around angry people? Found them not so friendly? A little standoffish? Untrusting? No smiles? Before you ask yourself, *Why is everyone treating me this way?* take a good long look at how you are treating them.

For remember—we reap what we sow.

tb Nature

This morning as I was on my way to church, the sky was filled with dark clouds. My husband and I began talking about how the weather forecaster had missed with the forecast. Saturday was to be the day of rain, while Sunday was to be a beautiful day with hardly a cloud.

Ooops. Saturday was the beautiful day with hardly a cloud, and Sunday started out as a day looming with dark, threatening clouds.

My thoughts turned to nature. When rain approaches, leaves will fold up to catch the rain. Animals will feel the barometric pressure change and seek shelter from upcoming storms and do so much quicker than humans will.

Even with today's technology, it is still more accurate to watch nature's forecast than the weather forecaster. Nature has never heard the forecast on TV, but it seems to know what weather is on its way. Nature knows when to cup those little leaves to drink the rain and when to take shelter from an incoming storm. Cool or what?

Why can nature forecast the weather far better than any weather forecaster without the use of modern technology?

Because nature listens to God.

tb Cisterns

> For my people have committed two evils: They have forsaken Me, the fountain of living waters, and hewn themselves cisterns—broken cisterns that can hold no water. (Jeremiah 2:13 NKJV)

Why is this a sin? It's because when you're digging your own cistern, you're in essence living life with your own strength. You're trying to dig your own cistern instead of letting God dig it for you. The cistern you are digging will not, cannot, be perfect like the one God can dig.

The cistern you dig will be broken and filled with holes and unable to hold God's promises or at least not many of them.

But if you allow God to dig your cistern, there will be

no holes in it and it will not only begin to be filled with God's promises but will be able to hold them as well.

What kind of promises? Promises like your salvation through Jesus. Like God's plans for you to live in hope. Like God will work all things for your good. Like God will hear your prayers and answer them.

You know—promises like that.

tb Drinking Water

My cat quickly laps water taking in small amounts with each lap. It's as if she's sipping the water. This required a lot of swallowing, a lot of work.

It was the dog's turn to drink from the same water bowl. The dog actually lapped up the water in a manner that allowed him to take in more water in less time and with less effort.

I thought about my horse and how she drinks water. She will actually submerge her entire muzzle in the water right up to her nostrils and suck in the water. She takes in very large amounts of water with very little effort.

The cat sipped. The dog lapped. The horse sucked. All three animals drank the water using different techniques for drinking, but they had one thing in common—they drank the water.

This makes me think about the different denominations— Baptist, Methodist, Lutheran, Church of God, Church of Christ, Church of the Nazarene, Presbyterian, and so on. Each service is different from the others.

Some of the churches are very conservative; they take in God's Word in small amounts. Like the cat, they sip.

Then we have churches that are very active and

boisterous. Like my horse, they suck in as much of God's Word as they can.

Somewhere in between are churches that are neither conservative nor boisterous. They tend to take in God's Word in steady amounts. They lap.

If all these churches are Bible-based churches filled with blood-washed, born-again believers who worship the Lord and Savior, Jesus Christ, believe in the Triune God, and believe the Bible is God's inerrant Word, they all have one thing in common. They drink the water. The Living Water.

Did not Jesus tell us that He is the Living Water? And that if any man would drink of the Living Water, he would never thirst again?

> Jesus answered and said to her, "Whoever drinks of this water will thirst again, but whoever drinks of the water that I shall give him will never thirst. But the water that I shall give him will become in him a fountain of water springing up into everlasting life." (John 4:13–14 NKJV)

Jesus said whoever drinks of the water—His Living water -be it Baptist, Methodist, Church of God, and so. Let us not judge the worship style of other churches. As long as they are Bible based, their services are filled with blood-washed, born-again believers worshipping Jesus Christ as their Savior and the one triune God. Who cares?

And if they aren't? Let's let God take care of that!

tb What a Picture

Two Sundays a month, my church provides church services for a nursing home. This may sound like wasted time, but most who attend the services are not able to go outside the facility much less to a church. Those who attend our services are knocking on death's door. And there may be some who have not asked Jesus to be their personal Savior and need to hear the gospel. So, from this point of view those who live in a nursing home are all sitting on the doorstep of either heaven or hell.

Having a true pastor's heart, my pastor preaches before the small crowd of wheelchairs as if he were preaching to a sanctuary filled to the brim. And in most of the wheelchairs sit people who are slumped over with mouth open and eyes closed. It is obvious that they are sleeping and could not care less about what they are hearing. Floating all around them in the air of the room is God's Word being proclaimed, and yet they are oblivious.

What a picture of how God's Word is being treated today in a world governed by Satan and his workers. People are slumped over with their mouths open demanding their right to do as they please. With their spiritual eyes closed, they are not caring about what they are hearing as the gospel is being preached over the airwaves in the form of radio, internet, e-mails, and tweets. Yes, they are obviously caught up in their own worlds and could not care less about anything that smells of righteousness.

How sad.

tb Our Permission?

When we pray, we often say, "If it is Your will, Lord" as if God needed our permission to do the things we are praying about. Or "in Your time, Lord" as if we are giving God our permission to do things when He wants to do them.

Jesus told us to pray in His name. At times, these phrases are said genuinely and with earnest hearts. At times in my prayer life, I seemed to be giving God permission to do what He wanted to do, when and how He wanted to do it, as if I were the boss dictating to God and God was my servant taking dictation on what I was praying about.

Really?

How arrogant of me to think I could tell almighty God how He should handle my prayer requests. How arrogant of me for trying to use God as my servant when I should be His servant taking dictation from Him.

How merciful of God for not taking me out when I try to be the boss. Thank you, Lord!

tb Glow of Lights

Last night while on our way home from Ocala, my husband's GPS routed us off I-75 for a while. We turned this way and that on small country roads known only by a number. And one of these roads turned out to be someone's driveway. *Arrg!*

As night fell, my concerns grew. We did not know the area we were in. We didn't even know the name of the area. All we knew is that we were just south of Ocala and well north of home.

However, we stayed the course the GPS had laid out for us, and then it happened. We saw a glow of lights in the distance—a city. The glow was in sharp contrast to the night sky and was a comfort. *Ah! There is hope that we will find our way back to I-75 after all.*

Hmmm.

This may be what Jesus's light looks like in the spiritual realm. There is darkness all around with souls trying to find their way. Then as the souls finally make that correct turn, they see it—light radiating from Jesus, their Savior, in stark contrast to the darkness and lostness in their lives.

What hope those souls find when they finally see the glow of Jesus's light. What comfort when they finally reach home and see Jesus in all His radiance face to face. What comfort when they reach

A place called heaven.

tb Second-Best Christmas Gift Ever

> But of that day and hour no one knows, not even the angels in heaven, nor the Son, but only the Father. Take heed, watch and pray; for you do not know when the time is. (Mark 13:32–33 NKJV)

No one knows when Jesus will come back for us. According to the above scripture, not even Jesus knows. Wouldn't it be the second-best Christmas ever if this Christmas Day was the day we heard a shout, the voice of an archangel, and the sound of God's trumpet announcing the coming of Jesus Christ? If this was the Christmas Day when the dead were caught up in the air and we who were alive followed? Think about it. Second-best Christmas ever.

The second-best Christmas ever? Really? Not the best?

The best Christmas Day was the birth of our Savior, who willingly spent time with us on earth. Yep! God's Son, Jesus Christ, is the best Christmas gift ever given to us on the best Christmas Day ever.

And the second-best Christmas gift ever will be when He returns for us, His church.

Yea!

tb Your Employer

In reality, God is your employer and you are His employee. Not sure about that? Let's look at it.

God has a plan for your life filled with work for you to do. God will instruct you how and when to do this work. He will give you the place and the opportunity to do it. He will provide the needed materials and finances to complete it.

Doesn't that sound like an employer?

God has given you a recipe for being successful at His work. There's no need to go to Harvard for an MBA. Just follow God's recipe for success.

God will reward you in ways your worldly employer never would be able to. You will find that sometimes, God's work is hard, exhausting, and demanding. But it is always rewarding.

And God's work will always get done. If you will not be a good employee and complete the task He has given you, He will find someone who will.

Ouch!

tb Someone's Watching You

Pick one thing and do it better than anyone else and you will be successful. I have heard this statement forever. Pick one thing and live it, eat it, breathe it, speak it, and dream it and you will have success. This is what the world tells us to do to be successful.

There are two things wrong with this philosophy. First off, it tells you that your success depends on you. And it does, but only up to a point. And the second thing is that it is a lie.

God's Word tells us of another way to be successful, the real way.

> And whatever you do, do it heartily, as to the Lord and not to men, knowing that from the Lord you will receive the reward of the inheritance; for you serve the Lord Christ. (Colossians 3:23–24 NKJV)

We are instructed to do our work with all our hearts. We are to do the best we can in a timely manner. We are to work to the best of our ability and not allow mediocrity to creep in. We are to work as if Jesus were physically there in the room with us looking over our shoulders and watching our every move.

We are to do all our work this way—work done in public and work done in private. Work that seems to be small and insignificant, and work that is large and important. All our work.

Remember that when you are working, Jesus is there with you. When you have done your work well, when you have turned in a good day's work for a day's wage, you are honoring God, and your employer will see your good work ethic and admire you for that. Your employer will see Jesus's teachings through your good work ethic.

And the bonus here is that if your employer does not appear to be someone who attends church, you have just given that person a sermon on how to serve Jesus without saying a word.

tb A Father's Love

Our interim pastor has been teaching from the book of Jonah. We all have read and heard about Jonah's rebellious ways toward God. About how his rebellion caused him to be swallowed by a big fish. About his prayers to God from the belly of that fish. And about the mercy God had for him.

Jonah was openly rebellious to God. He did not want to do what God had asked him to do. So he decided to run away from God and hide out.

Really? How can you hide from God? God is everywhere; He sees all and knows all. So where could you go?

Though Jonah eventually did as God had asked him, he did so with protest in his heart. He did not have warm fuzzies in his heart for the work God wanted him to do as he went to Nineveh. Jonah was probably rolling his eyes as he traveled to that town. He was still being rebellious, and God rebuked Jonah verbally.

But there's another side to this story, one that shows God's mercy and love.

Jonah was disobedient to God, so God placed him in the belly of a big fish. A type of time-out if you will. While in his time-out, Jonah started pleading with God for help and mercy. In essence, Jonah was crying out, "I'm sorry, Daddy! I won't do it again!" In His great love and mercy, God heard and answered his pleas.

We have all heard those words from our children. We all can remember how those cries for mercy tugged at our heartstrings. How hard it was to make our children serve their full sentences in time-out.

God is all powerful; He could have just sucked the breath right out of Jonah's lungs, but He didn't. God, Jonah's heavenly Father, was patient with him. He rebuked Jonah when it was necessary, but He followed it up with mercy and love.

God does the same in all our lives. He will rebuke us if we need it. But when we have repented for our disobedience truly, honestly, and earnestly, He will have mercy on us and shower us with His love.

By the way, don't be too hard on the Ninevites in your life. We all have been someone's Ninevite at some time or other.

tb Living by God's Rules

If only we would live by the rules God set for us in the Bible. Life would be so much better and less costly as well.

First off, we all would work hard. There would be no need for welfare. Those who did not work would not eat.

> For even when we were with you, we commanded you this: If anyone will not work, neither shall he eat. (2 Thessalonians 3:10 NKJV)

Then we would give the first 10 percent of our gross income, not 10 percent of what was left over, to God's church. Then God's storehouse could be filled with necessary items needed by those who cannot work and for the widows. And we would share with each other generously.

> Bring all the tithes into the storehouse, that there may be food in My house, and try Me now in this," says the LORD of hosts, "If I will not open for you the windows of heaven and pour out for you such blessing that there will not be room enough to receive it. (Malachi 3:10 NKJV)

Third, living by God's rules would eliminate the need for government welfare as we would be taking care of our own. Without the need for government welfare, we would have no need for welfare offices and their expenses, which would lower our taxes. We would have more to live on. And we could then give even more to God's storehouse.

If only we would live by God's rules.

tb Worship Like a Tree

All nature worships God. Look at how the grass, the flowers, the shrubs, and the trees grow. Small trees will actually grow around larger ones so they too can reach the sky. So that they can stretch their limbs up towards the sun. Up towards heaven.

We, the only creation God made in His image, is the one creation that often looks down and away from the sky.

Away from the Son. Away from heaven. How sad it must make God to see His image looking away from Him. Yet because of His great mercy, He keeps waiting for the day when we will all look up to the Son. To heaven. To Him.

Where are you looking? Are your limbs stretching up to the Son? To heaven? Do your eyes look up? It's much easier to see God when you're looking up.

Don't let nature do all the worshipping! Do what the trees are doing—throw your head up, stretch out your hands, and sing praises to our Lord with all that's in you. Thank Him for His mercy and patience. Thank Him for the immeasurable love He has for you. Thank Him for Jesus, your sacrificial sin Lamb. And thank Jesus for His obedience to the cross.

Feel the warmth of His love, the warmth of Jesus's blood covering you and washing you clean from your sins. Feel His newness of life.

Now that's worship!

> Let everything that has breath praise the LORD. Praise the LORD! (Psalm 150:6 NKJV)

tb What If God Visited You?

The Old Testament is filled with people who had visits from God. Abraham. Isaac. Moses. Gideon. Joshua. Those are only a few. While most of these men received their instructions verbally, Moses's experience was that of actually being in the presence of God. What a privilege!

Can you imagine what would happen today if God visited with you as He did with Moses in the Old Testament? One night as you are spending quiet time reading your

Bible, a brilliant light comes down from heaven into your living room. The light is so bright that drivers on your street can no longer see where they are going and have to pull over. Your neighbors close their blinds tight in an attempt to block out the blinding light. They may even grumble some because your heavenly light is interfering with their ability to watch TV.

Air traffic controllers see your bright light as a blip on their radar screens. They're trying to figure out what this blip is and where it came from. Not finding answers to their questions, they report the blip to the air force, which scrambles F-15s to your address.

Fire and Rescue show up because someone called 911 and reported a bomb going off at your address. The FBI, CIA, and Homeland Security show up; they want to see what's going on firsthand.

Think of all the chaos your heavenly light is causing in your small part of the world. Think of all the people running around filled with anxiety and fear. News crews are all over your yard and your neighbor's. Helicopters are flying over while reporters report live about a strange light coming from the skies into your house.

This brilliant light spills out of your windows and illuminates the surrounding area. Frightened people start rumors. Could this light be aliens contacting you? Are they taking you up to the mother ship?

Then you step out of your home radiating the light of God, a light that is so bright that no one can cast their eyes on you. Bio Haz-Med Control is called out. You must be contaminated with something from aliens maybe? And if your contamination is not from aliens, it must be due to radiation, a nuclear bomb perhaps? What else could explain the bright light that filled your house and now radiates from you?

Maybe a visit from God?

Do you think the world would believe you if you were to say you had just been in the presence of God? That the light radiating from you is not the light of aliens but the light of God?

Oh this poor world!

Even if God did come down from heaven to visit as He did in Moses's day, this world would not believe it. People would miss out on something spectacular. Almighty God could be standing there for all the world to see and no one would believe it was God. People would think they were looking at an alien.

How sad.

tb Is It Still God's Promise?

> When I shut up heaven and there is no rain, or command the locusts to devour the land, or send pestilence among My people, if My people who are called by My name will humble themselves and pray and seek My face, and turn from their wicked ways, then I will hear from heaven, and will forgive their sin and heal their land. (2 Chronicles 7:13–14 NKJV)

I have been told that this verse and others like it such as Jeremiah 29:11 are commonly taken out of context and used incorrectly. That this promise and others in the Old Testament were for the Israelites of the Old Testament, who were being rebellious and had turned from God. I understand what my brother in Christ was saying.

However, I believe that all God's promises in the Old and New Testaments are for all His people. People who lived then. People who live now. And people who will live in the future.

God said "if My people"—if *My* people. God's Word also tells us that the moment I accepted His Son, Jesus Christ, as my Savior, the moment I repented and turned from my wicked ways, I became His child, one of His people. At the moment I was sealed with His seal, even though I am a Gentile, I was grafted into the nation of Israel, God's nation.

I don't know if I use this scripture out of context or not, but I wholeheartedly believe it's a promise God gave me. I believe that all God's Word—His promises and everything—were given to all His children regardless of when or where they live.

And I am one of His children.

tb Do You Have Instincts?

Needing more barn cats, we allowed our young female to have a litter of kittens before we spayed her. What an amazing mommy she turned out to be.

She delivered four kittens, removed the one that was stillborn, cleaned up the live ones, and began to feed them. All by herself. No doctors. No midwives. No hospital stays. No how-to-have-babies books. Just her all by herself in a quiet corner of my home. She instinctively knew how to deliver her babies, how to clean them up, how to feed them, and how to love them. It was as if God had given her instructions on how to do these things. And she listened.

I believe animals have not lost their ability to listen to God and do as He instructs them. We call it instinct.

Yet I, a human being, someone made in the image of God, tend not to listen to and do as God tells me to. No! I tend to question God. "Is that really You, God? Do you really want me to do that, God? That way, God? Am I really to go there, God? Are You sure, God? Me, God?"

But God placed inside all of us a still, small voice. The moment we accept Jesus Christ as our personal sin Lamb, we receive the Holy Spirit to dwell in us; our bodies become temples of the Holy Spirit.

> Or do you not know that your body is the temple of the Holy Spirit who is in you, whom you have from God, and you are not your own? For you were bought at a price; therefore glorify God in your body and in your spirit, which are God's. (1 Corinthians 6:19–20 NKJV)

Sometimes, we choose not to listen to the Holy Spirit. Or we allow others' voices and the sounds of our world to clutter our minds and distract us from God's voice.

We tend to always have background noise as we go about our day. Just walk into the waiting room or the lobby of a professional and you will hear music. At home, we tend to listen to something be it the radio or something else.

If you were to watch animals, you would see they rarely walk into a room and turn on a radio or a TV. Instead, they spend countless hours being quiet and still. Perhaps we all could learn something from our furry friends. Like the art of being still before the Lord.

Maybe we should start being quiet and still before God more often. Maybe, just maybe, if we did that, we could hear God's voice and live God's way. Maybe we too could live by instinct.

> Be still and know that I am God; I will be exalted among the nations, I will be exalted in the earth! (Psalm 46:10 NKJV)

tb Be a Dog

One pleasant afternoon, I spent time outside with my dog. She ran around the grassy yard sniffing here and there. Then she laid in the grass and rolled over on her back. With her legs in the air, she squirmed in the grass. When that was done, she laid on her side and rubbed her face in the grass. Oh what fun she was having and how happy she looked. The sight of her enjoyment made me snicker. Her joy made me happy.

Then a thought came to me. If it makes me happy to see my dog enjoying something I have provided her, it must make my Lord happy to see me enjoying what He has given me. Things like pets, a home, a church, a husband, and yes, even horses.

Are you enjoying the things the Lord has provided for you? Are you lying on your back with your legs in the air squirming around in the grassy yards God has given to you?

No? Then please start. Can't you see in your mind's eye just how big God's smile is when He sees you enjoying what He has given you?

tb Did I Really Mean Those Words?

While going through a very difficult time, I felt God had turned His back on me and had walked away. I felt betrayed, confused, alone, and unloved. My mind told me that God had promised to always be with me and to never forsake me, but my heart told me otherwise.

I cried out to God. Spent time in His Word. Prayed night and day. But still, the trial stayed and even became worse.

Reaching the point of desperation, I thought that perhaps from this moment on I should live for me, not God. That perhaps I should do whatever I had to do to get out of this trial no matter what it was.

The trial I was facing guaranteed public disgrace, financial hardship, and the loss of friends. To add insult to injury, the trial was caused by something I had not created. It was something I had had no control over. Something that was not a consequence of my actions or my fault.

I felt God was not listening to me anyway. At least, that is how it seemed. Or maybe even worse, that God was listening but did not care.

Arrg! God! Where are You? Why have You deserted me? Why do you not care?

Wait a minute. That must have been the way Jesus felt in the garden on the night of His arrest. He had lived solely for God. Everything He had done or said was what God had wanted Him to do or say. Jesus's only motive in life was to please His Heavenly Father. And yet while in the garden, when He prayed to His Heavenly Father asking—no, begging—for God to provide another way, it may have seemed God didn't care about what happened to Him.

When Jesus was hanging on the cross naked for all to see, battered, and bruised, He must have felt His Heavenly Father had turned from Him and walked away.

How often have I sang, "I have decided to follow Jesus, no turning back"? Do I mean those words? Can I live with no other purpose or motive than to please my Heavenly Father? Am I able to walk the same road Jesus walked?

Yes, this trial I am facing guarantees great public shame, lonely times, financial hardship, and disappointment.

But the trial Jesus faced brought Him death.

tb The Candle

While cleaning, I lit a scented candle. I like a nice-smelling home. *Hmmm.* The spiced-apple aroma began to flow throughout my house giving it a warm, cozy atmosphere. Continuing with my cleaning, I went into the next room for a few minutes.

When I returned to the room where the candle was burning I realized the spiced-apple aroma was no longer happening. I saw that the flame was flickering wildly around the wick. It appeared to have a mind of its own and was reaching above the jar's rim.

Upon a closer look, I saw something that looked like a cross. Yes. The fire closest to the wick had formed a cross while the misbehaving outer flames were dancing around the wick. Swirling this way and that as if they were trying to destroy the cross.

Watching this scenario reminded me of how Satan is a flame that misbehaves. He flickers and swirls around the crosses in our hearts and tries to destroy them. I was reminded of how I needed to make sure my cross-formed wick was well cared for. And that I had to put on my full armor of God daily if not hourly or minute by minute to make sure I had full protection from Satan's fiery darts.

While it was easy for me to snuff out the flames of a candle, it is not easy for me to snuff out Satan's flames. Only the blood of Jesus can do that.

tb Doomsday Dave

One night, I watched a *Twilight Zone* episode that seemed to have been written during the height of the nuclear bomb scare era. I can remember as a very young girl having bomb drills in elementary school. We were instructed to get under our desks. Like that would protect us from a nuclear bomb?

This episode was about Dave, someone who continually warned his neighbors of an upcoming nuclear attack. For some reason that was never revealed, Dave had some inside information about nuclear bombs being dropped on his neighborhood.

With genuine concern for his neighbors, he tried to convince them of the threat. He tried to tell them they should build bomb shelters in their basements and stock them with food and water. But his neighbors only laughed at him. They called him Doomsday Dave.

That is until the alarms went off. The same neighbors who had made fun of Doomsday Dave when he told them to build bomb shelters ran to his house. They had not listened to Doomsday Dave; they had not built bomb shelters as Doomsday Dave had.

They wanted Dave to let them into his bomb shelter, but it was big enough only for his family. Though they pleaded with him to let them in, Dave had to turn his neighbors away.

His neighbors with whom he had pleaded to build bomb shelters were banging on his shelter's door shouting angrily and pleading for their lives. But Dave could not let them in. To do so would have been a death sentence for his family.

Dave had warned his neighbors over and over, but no one had listened to him. It was too late for them.

The story made me think of Noah and the ark. As the waters rose and the dry land decreased, were his neighbors hanging onto the sides of the ark? Banging on it? Pleading for their lives?

And how did Noah feel hearing those he had warned over and over again, pleading with him to let them in?

Noah could not open the door. That would have been a direct violation of God's Word.

And Noah's first obligation was to obey God.

tb Our Great Provider

God is so good to us. He has provided ways for us—our bodies and minds—to have good physical, mental, and spiritual health.

During summer, some of us have bodies that hold onto excess water. It's also a time when watermelons grow. And watermelons are natural diuretics. *Hmmm.*

During the winter, when our sun is not as strong, we find our bodies require an increase in vitamins C and D. It is also during the winter that citrus fruits grow. Oranges and their cousins are extremely high in vitamin C. *Hmmm.*

Need one more example?

At times, we feel stressed out from a day of nonstop demands. Or maybe from watching too much 11:00 p.m. news. When you are in one of those times, rub lavender oil on your hands and allow the aroma to fill your senses. It has a calming effect on the body and mind. Relaxation without drugs. *Hmmm.*

Isn't God wonderful?

tb My Sister's Granddaughter

My sister's two-month-old granddaughter was cranky and restless. Being unable to tell us what was wrong, all she could do was cry. And cry she did.

All that my sister and I could do was guess the reason for her crying. And guess we did.

As a two-month-old, her world centered on her wants and needs, which were usually one of five things—a nap, pain, hunger, thirst, or dry diapers. And we adults have to tend to those needs to the best of our ability.

My sister and I eventually found the baby's problem and quickly attended to it. Once the problem was gone, the baby was smiling and cooing and responding to love. Yes! Even at two months, the baby would respond to love. When my sister talked to her, the girl would smile and kick her feet and shake her hands. She obviously liked being loved on. That in turn made us smile back.

Baby Christians are the same. Our Bibles tell us that they can take in only milk and that they tend to be self-centered. They also need to be tended to, and sometimes, they need to be carried.

> For though by this time you ought to be teachers, you need someone to teach you again the first principles of the oracles of God; and you have come to need milk and not solid food. For everyone who partakes only of milk is unskilled in the word of righteousness, for he is a babe. But solid food belongs to those who are of full age, that is, those who by reason of use have their senses exercised to discern both good and evil. (Hebrews 5:12–14 NKJV)

But as they grow into mature Christians, their meals are more fortifying and their focus shifts from their needs to the needs of others.

Mature Christians have the responsibility of tending to baby Christians to the best of their ability.

We will find that just as that baby did, our baby Christians will respond to love in a positive way. We will find that they like to be talked to and be loved on. Just like with that baby girl, we will find that the smiles on our baby Christians' faces will make us smile back.

tb Abraham and Isaac

Have you ever wondered if Abraham could have gone to the mountain to sacrifice his promised son, Isaac, because he had faith that the Lord would provide another sacrificial lamb at the last minute?

Or could it be that Abraham believed that the Lord was merciful and powerful enough to breathe life back into Isaac's dead body?

And what about Isaac? If Abraham had not followed through on God's request, if he had not gone all the way and done as God had asked him to, Isaac would not have witnessed a miracle firsthand. Isaac would not have been part of God's miracle and would not have seen how merciful and loving God is.

Because of his father's great obedience to God, Isaac learned firsthand how faithful God is, that he could always trust God, and that God's way is always the best way. By following God's will, Abraham impacted Isaac's life forever.

Our actions impact others. Our obedience or disobedience to God will impact those who we come in contact with. Through our obedience to God, others may see that God is faithful, trustworthy, merciful, and loving. And that God's way is always the best way.

Hmmm. Chew on that for a while.